D1621878

To my dear Jill,

Ghost Dance
in Berlin

A Rhapsody in Gray

who made a home
for my words

5 March 2013

Ghost Dance in Berlin

A Rhapsody in Gray

Peter Wortsman

Travelers' Tales
an imprint of Solas House, Inc.
Palo Alto

Copyright © 2013 Peter Wortsman. All rights reserved.

All interior photographs by Peter Wortsman © 2013.

Travelers' Tales and Solas House are trademarks of Solas House, Inc., 2320 Bowdoin Street, Palo Alto, California 94306, www.travelerstales. com

Production Editor: Christy Quinto
Page Layout: Cynthia Lamb, using the font Janson MT
Cover Design: Kimberly N. Coombs
Cover Photographs: Peter Wortsman; Reichstag Dome, Berlin © Vangelis
Author Photograph: Jean-Luc Fievet

ISBN: 978-1-60952-078-6 (pbk.)

Distributed by Publishers Group West, 1700 Fourth Street, Berkeley, California 94710.

Library of Congress Cataloging-in-Publication Data pending

First Edition
Printed in the United States
10 9 8 7 6 5 4 3 2 1

To Claudie, Jacques, and Aurélie, my beloved fellow travelers,
And to the memory of Alfred and Dora Wortsman

Berlin comprises, first, the bequest of untold dead, and second, the doings of the living.

—ALFRED DÖBLIN

CONTENTS

FOREWORD

The last time I visited Berlin I made eye contact with the most beautiful woman in the world, only she was stone-hearted and more than four thousand years old, and didn't speak a word of English or German, or any other living tongue. I looked her up again not long ago but she had moved. Displaced from the banks of the Nile to a palace in Charlottenburg, and from there to the Museumsinsel in the Spree, she'd changed lodgings yet again from the Altes to the recently resurrected Neues Museum, where she finally found a room of her own, her elusive look locked forever in a glass case on the edge of a smile. This being Berlin, all bets are on where Frau Nefertiti will turn up next.

Next door in the Pergamon Museum the packaged remains of several empires are pickled and preserved, including a section of the walls of Babylon and a scale model of the ill-fated Tower of Babel, the World Trade Center of antiquity, downed by an angry deity. It's a hop, skip, and a jump to the site of the old *Stadtschloß*, once an emperor's urban residence, flattened by Allied bombing and post-War ideological bulldozers, now a hole in the heart of the city. It's a stone's throw from there to the TV Tower at Alexanderplatz, the obsolete symbol of another lost illusion formerly upheld with a since-fallen wall. But the traffic rushes on and pedestrians throng the stately thoroughfare Unter den Linden, at the tail end of which the old Brandenburg Gate is open for business again.

Built on a heap of urban impulses, Berlin is a phoenix forever being reborn. Eight centuries old, it has managed with an uncanny resilience to remain ever young by reinventing itself time and again to suit an ever-changing geopolitical reality.

A city in constant flux, very much like New York, Berlin has kept reinventing itself, while going through makeover after makeover: primped up from provincial backwater to Prussian seat of government; built up by Bismarck into the Biedermeier Hohenzollern Imperial Hauptstadt, only to be deconstructed, upon the empire's sudden collapse, into the short-lived Weimar Republican fever-dream of modernity and capital of the avant-garde; enshrined as grandiose Thousand-Year Reichstadt and redubbed Germania, only to be reduced a few years later to an occupied and divided rubble heap at the fault line of history; revived in a schizoid state of post-World War II duality; reunited and redefined yet again in 1989 when the Wall came tumbling down.

Like New York, I think of Berlin not as a proper noun, but rather as a "proper," albeit transitive, verb—with a mass transit(ive) system that actually works—forever evolving, boomeranging, or *"Berlining"* (*sich Berlinernd*) into the city of tomorrow. With the flow of traffic regulated (symbolically at least) by the replica of the original traffic light—Europe's first—at Potsdamer Platz, *es Berlinert sich immer weiter...* It keeps right on *"Berlining."*

I myself have witnessed the city's dizzying metamorphoses over the last four decades.

First, at a gathering of Fulbright Fellows in 1973, when the divisions of East and West, emblematic of the split in the world, literally cast in cement, seemed insurmountable.

Next, to visit a friend in the East in 1986, on his thirty-ninth birthday, coincidentally the twenty-fifth anniversary of the erection of the *Antifaschistischer Schutzwall* (Anti-Fascist Protective Dike), as it was officially referred to in the German Democratic Republic (GDR). When, in a post office in East Berlin, I wanted to purchase a copy of the commemorative stamp marking a quarter century of protection against the perceived fascist threat to the west, the heretofore poker-faced woman at the service window actually burst out laughing, convinced that I was kidding, and I had to repeat my request a second time before, with a look of utter amazement, she slipped me the sticky, perforated image. No one had ever asked for the stamp.

And that was a mere three years before a hunk of the demolished Berlin Wall sold as a hot collector's item at Macy's in New York.

Then, in the summer of 2007, I walked along a line of bricks, an urban scar in the pavement near Checkpoint Charlie, that marked (and mocked) the erstwhile division where the Wall once stood. And from the glass dome bulging like a prescient eye atop the renovated Reichstag Building I saw the restless cranes of progress yet again reconfiguring the idea of a city.

Filmmaker Walter Ruttmann captured the restless rush in his 1927 documentary montage, *Berlin: Die Sinfonie der Großstadt* (Berlin: Symphony of a Metropolis), in which legs and arms take on a life of their own and motion is the primary emotion. Novelist Alfred Döblin used a similar montage technique to mine the city's ever-excitable subconscious, painting its fluid portrait in his epic novel *Berlin Alexanderplatz*, published in 1929. At around the same time Georg Grosz's penciled and painted grotesques likewise caught the crazy rhythm, and Kurt Weill and Friedrich Holländer sounded its sultry jazz riffs in songs interpreted by Lotte Lenya and Marlene Dietrich, until the music was silenced and the dance forced into lockstep by booted storm troopers.

But the city's indomitable spirit survived, and here I am again, still waiting for Nefertiti to blink.

1

My *Winterreise*

*C*HEWING ON A MOUTHFUL BIT OFF A HALF LOAF OF
coarse *Vollkorn* (whole grain) bread bought bright and
early when the baker at the S-Bahn Station Berlin-
Wannsee opened for business, I am standing, knee-deep
in snow, at the grave of writer Heinrich von Kleist, on a
wooded knoll overlooking the Kleiner Wannsee (Little

Wann Lake), where, with a pistol shot, the troubled Romantic put a last period on the sentence of his life. The warm dough kneaded between tongue and palate and the kernels exploding under the millstone of my molars make for a pleasant distraction from the cold, an inner armor that insulates and fortifies. Nobody knows how to bake whole grain bread like the Germans, it tastes like it just came out of the oven in "Hänsel and Gretel."

Shooting up out of sleep at daybreak, thrilled to be alive, I waited for the darkness to dissolve before venturing out, bundled up, a walking seven-layer cake, wadded with boxers and T-shirt, long johns, flannel shirt, sweater, overcoat, hat, hood, and woolen scarf, reveling in the frozen silence.

The spectacle of the icy lake glimpsed through the blurry periscope of my tearing eyes is dreamlike, birds frozen in flight and sailboats iced in at half-tilt. The pillow of snow on the lonesome tombstone supplants the white hair Kleist, a suicide at thirty-four, never lived to grow. It's a peaceful, melancholy spot removed from the road in a copse of evergreens—not quite as remote as Kleist must have found it, but almost. Hard to imagine it's still within Berlin's city limits. An unassuming carved wooden sign, easy to miss unless you're looking for it, points toward a winding footpath, oddly discouraging access. I am the only living soul in sight, and though I understand they mean to make it more presentable by 2011, the bicentennial of his passing, for the moment at least it's still conducive to musing.

The poet Rilke went to Paris to serve as secretary to the sculptor Rodin and managed to carve a memorable book from the experience.[1] Secretary, in a manner of speaking, to Kleist—it's my English take on his words that helped earn me this sojourn in Berlin[2]—he would surely not have begrudged my extracting a few reflections.

---

[1] *The Notebooks of Malte Laurids Brigge*, Rainer Maria Rilke, Paris: 1910

[2] *Selected Prose of Heinrich von Kleist*, selected, translated and with an afterword by Peter Wortsman, Archipelago Books, New York: 2010

Wannsee, the posh district of lakeside villas where I live, is named for the lakes. The Academy is considerably less intimidating than I had feared.[3] The white wine helps. The nicest thing about it is the silence and the solitude when I want it, and then to emerge for limited spells of sociability at breakfast and dinner.

★

Gazing at me over the rim of his glasses, the bookkeeper at the Academy, to whom I'd come to inquire regarding the delay in the payment of my monthly stipend, caught me peering out the window at the Großer (Big) Wannsee, the vast frozen body of water out back, perhaps divining my intent. "It's not really a lake, you know, it's a swollen river," he remarked with a clipped, nervous laugh, adding, "People have fallen in." The poet Georg Heym, another casualty of German letters, fell through a hole in the ice. But this is my year of living dangerously, the coldest winter in decades. When the young women on staff dare do it, as they say they will, I too will walk across.

---

[3] The American Academy in Berlin, where the author resided as Holtzbrinck Fellow in the spring of 2010

*

Wintry Berlin is a city largely devoid of color, except for a dirty white carpet of snow flung over a treacherous ice slick and a perennial gray cloud cover overhead, ice and sky running into each other, stained by the faint yellow trace of a distant sun that never quite breaks through.

*

Picture my surprise last Wednesday on my way back to Wannsee, at the sight of a green hand gripping the railing before me on the crowded tram and artificial ruby-red hair flapping in a simulated tropical breeze. Part wildebeest, part uprooted palm tree escaping the inhospitable arctic chill into the hothouse on wheels. And in the startling blur—a sudden burst of color blinds—the green gloved hands became fluttering palm leaves and the electric redhead a fabulous fruit, a cross between a pineapple, a coconut, and a ripe pomegranate—more tantalizing and forbidding than Eve's fabled apple of temptation. In vain did my nostrils flutter in search of an olfactory rush, for this exotic fruit had no scent. She was cold, an ice fairy, a Berlin mirage, dashing out ahead of me at Alexanderplatz, and promptly melting, the renegade burst of color immediately blending back into the ubiquitous gray.

★

Sunday, despite the sub-zero temperature, I trekked the considerable distance out to Charlottenburg Palace—Berlin is a vast urban expanse—to catch the closing of the Lucas Cranach exhibit. I admit to an erotic tingle at the sight of all those oddly titillating blond nudes: his quizzical Eve, fondling fig leaf and apple; a seductive Teutonic Venus engaged in a sultry bump and grind with a veil that reveals more than it hides; bold Judith, sword in hand outside the tent, just after beheading Holofernes; and the virtuous Lady Lucretia, all her soon-to-be self-sacrificed loveliness on display, preferring death to dishonor—the pin-up girls of antiquity priming and pricking burgeoning Protestant morality. But I was particularly taken by the small self-portrait of the painter, a personal friend of Luther, who, despite his considerable worldly success, opted to preserve this guilt-ridden gaze to pass on to posterity. My libido too numb to take the tingle along, Cranach's uneasy look accompanied me on my chilly rush home.

At minus ten degrees Celsius, the frigid sunset over Alexanderplatz, where I emerged from the U-Bahn (subway) to catch the S-Bahn (elevated), made the ground feel like a glacier underfoot. There on the frozen pavement sat a hooded black man playing pipes. Not bagpipes, mind you, massive metal pipes, a makeshift instrument composed of lead fittings twisted pretzel-like and painted blue, on which he banged a primal rhythm and blew a ululating wail, a cross between the guttural groan of an aboriginal didgeridoo and the mournful lament of a landlocked leviathan still aching with life while divining imminent death. His *Lied der Kälte* (Song of the Cold) echoed in the arctic chill, each frozen note an inkling of eternity. Too cold to pull off my gloves, reach into my pocket, and pluck out a coin, I rushed by, stirred by the sound, wondering how long he'd have enough breath and dexterity left in his frozen fingers to keep blowing and banging.

Oblivious, meanwhile, to such rarefied aesthetic considerations, two homeless men, the one without gloves pushing the other, without legs, along in a rickety wheelchair with one wheel broken, the protruding spokes flicking a curious percussive accompaniment, went whizzing by to seek the tenuous shelter of the un-heated station. Wintry Berlin is no place for beggars. From the corner of my eye I caught the legless one in the wheelchair shrugging at the musician, as if to say: He's still got all his limbs, so what's he wailing about? Or perhaps it was a grudging shrug of sympathy. Too cold to consider for long, we almost collided, exchanging chilly looks, and each rushed off to our separate destinies.

2

The Vectors of Alexanderplatz

BERLINERS FONDLY CALL IT "ALEX" FOR SHORT, LIKE IT was an old friend with a familiar, pudgy, pockmarked face, a perennial beer buzz, and a couple of front teeth missing. That mangy mug has undergone multiple facelifts over the years, and given the prodigious bulge of its cheeks, and the various pockets or forecourts it encompasses, it is hard to say just where Alex ends and the rest of Berlin begins. And in a sense it hardly matters, since Alex is as much a state of mind as a precise locale. There's nothing beautiful about it. In fact, it's really rather ugly, as far as urban spaces go, compared to the great monumental squares of Paris, London, and Rome. But Alexanderplatz is positively electric, pure current unmediated by wires. Rumbling with arriving and departing underground and above-ground trains, trams, taxis, and buses, clip-clopping with boots, it's not a place to linger for long.

Busy as it is, with its central space comprising a vast pedestrian mall, a virtual skating rink perennially frozen in winter, swarming with visitors and locals once it thaws, zigzagged by bikers and pedestrians rushing every which way, ringed by streetcar tracks that tear up the pavement like a giant zipper, a shapeless train station, and a slew of unsightly department stores, with a Socialist era TV Tower rearing up like an unruly tuft of hair—still something about it radiates congeniality. A certain indomitable spirit has survived the ravages of time and war, regime and fashion changes, and the successive priorities of Wilhelmine, Weimar, Fascist, Socialist, and Capitalist urban planning, squeezing an enduring gaiety out of this shapeless hub of humanity smack dab in the middle of this sprawling city, of which it is a bulbous microcosm.

The erstwhile Ochsenplatz (Oxen Square) located just outside the gates of medieval Berlin was rechristened Königstor Platz (King's Gate Square) to mark the crowning of Prussian King Friedrich I in 1701, subsequently subdivided into a military parade ground and a fairground, and thereafter rejoined and redubbed Alexanderplatz by Emperor Friedrich Wilhelm III in honor of the ceremonial visit of his arch-rival Russian Czar Alexander I in 1805.

But Alex was too rowdy to remain royal for long.

Here at the crossroads of countless urban currents, the DNA of the future was spun in the double helix of politics and economics. Street battles were pitched in the March Revolution of 1848. The foundations of the former royal fortress were broken through and dug out to form the bed of the elevated S-Bahn, a veritable revolution in mass transit, opened to considerable fanfare in 1882. Department stores tapped the commercial potential of this sprawling perimeter, luring the ebb and flood of mass consumption until the money ran out. Here the murdered revolutionaries Karl Liebknecht and Rosa Luxemburg were mourned by a mass assembly in 1919, and the communist KPD and the socialist USPD joined forces a year later to battle it out with the bourgeois establishment.

Satirist Kurt Tucholsky embraced the space in "Total Manoli," his 1920 cabaret song: *"Weil diese Zeit fiebert und schreit, wackeln alle Wände."* (Because this moment fevers and screams, all the walls tremble). Experimental filmmaker Walter Ruttmann shot much of the electrifying footage of his 1927 documentary, *Berlin: Symphony of a Metropolis,* within its seething, swelling circumference. Author Alfred Döblin recalibrated its modern human and inhuman vectors in his epic novel *Berlin Alexanderplatz*, published in 1929, situating it at the beating heart of the twenties.

Lost Berliners still get their bearings by looking up and catching a glimpse of the spire of the TV Tower, that erstwhile Socialist symbol of the German Democratic Republic conceived in 1964 and completed in 1971 to goad the bourgeois burghers in the Western sector. And then in 1989, Alexanderplatz, East Berlin's answer to Moscow's Red Square, was the site of the mass demonstration, some five hundred thousand strong, that finally brought down the system and the Wall. The TV Tower has since changed colors, so to speak, converted from red beacon into an all-purpose symbol of German unity, the ungainly needle tailor-made for the button-hole of the reopened Brandenburg Gate.

Weather permitting, the rowdy punks who congregate indoors in the S-Bahn station through the long winter, drinking beer, insulting passersby, and jostling with police, spill out onto the esplanade. Here where unsavory spies and party apparatchiks once mingled with fresh-faced Young Pioneers, sausage salesman with portable ovens wrapped around their middle and flimsy parasols flapping in the wind now hawk their savory wares.

If you don't watch out, you'll forget yourself and where you're going and get gobbled up, for Alex is an ogre with a bottomless appetite.

3

Erinnerungen/ Remembering

THE OLD MAN WITH THE BABY CARRIAGE I ENCOUNTERED the other day on the S-Bahn Station platform at Alexanderplatz was a doting grandfather, I thought, until I bent forward to admire the baby, and saw that he was, in fact, wheeling his own childhood about. There was nothing stirring in the stroller between today's rubbish and yesterday's crumpled news but the devastation of regret. Surely he must've been headed somewhere, but hesitating on the edge of the platform, pivoting and pirouetting—contemplating suicide perhaps—he peered into the distance, then glanced at a non-existent wristwatch. Like all other commuters, it was for him, too, a matter of time, arrival and departure, but not according to the same schedule. Drunken, mad, or both, he was headed back to a never completely lapsed present, a time and place others abandon to the past, but which remained a suspended tense for him, though he couldn't tell from which way it was coming. With his gray mess of hair and wild gaze looking like a troubled twin of Einstein, that other sometime Berliner, this old man spun his own theory of relativity, a telling equation linking time and space with the elusive flash of memory squared.

*

How vividly do I still remember my father's face—dead and gone more than three decades now—back in New York, home from his first return trip to the Old Country. It was 1959, I was seven, and he appeared midday like a

G-Man in a dark business suit, an angel-agent come to release me from the holding cell of Miss O'Donohugh's second grade class, and take me home.

In my memory I badly need to pee, but don't dare ask, lest she refuse permission, as she often did, so I am doubly grateful for this deliverance. At first sight I don't recognize his physiognomy; the eyebrows are too arched, the forehead wrinkled, the lips pursed, though I know it's him from the sweetness of the smile and the scent of Odol, his German mouthwash. He's consumed by conflicting emotions, shaken, unhinged and elated, in the aftermath of having set foot again on the streets of his native Vienna after so many years. Like Berlin, Vienna too was reduced to a rubble heap. Love, longing, and regret battle it out in his otherwise mild expression, as he struggles to communicate to his young son the experience of return.

At seven, I don't understand, and perhaps will never fathom, what it means to have the world swept out from under your feet, all sense of certainty dissolved, the here and now transformed in a flash and forever into a there and then, to leave, like Lot, on the run, with your back to the flames, and then to return half a lifetime later to the once familiar scene, now reduced to a million-piece

Ravensburger puzzle only partially reassembled, with many more pieces missing than found. A refugee turned traveler, the restless heritage he bequeathed to me.

But what matters the most to me at the time are the German-made toy soldiers he brings back as a gift, hand-painted plastic medieval knights with fierce expressions, at once far more realistic and far more fantastic than my army of anonymous green plastic GIs, the latter too recent in association to allow for the license of fantasy.

Almost immediately they become my favorite playthings, these painted knights and the catapults, battering rams, and other siege equipment that come with them. (Germans still make the best soldiers.)

To my father, these figurines are the incarnation of that afternoon on his veranda in Vienna, so often told and retold, when he was seven or thereabouts, and riveted by the cavalcade of men in armor who suddenly came riding by on horseback, shot by cameramen on wheels for a long-forgotten silent film, circa 1921—though I could probably track it down on the internet, the great collective lost and found of misplaced impressions—the experience that engraved itself in his consciousness and simultaneously burnt itself into his skin with a sunburn that sent him feverish to bed. It's a silent film onto which he later spliced endless reels of us, his faithful little crew, marching with painted-on 1950s smiles toward a sweet future that has since faded into a bittersweet past.

And mingled with that remembered pageant, piggybacking upon it, my father must also have preserved the somber memory of another army led by the man with the little round mustache, an Austrian like himself, whose troops came goose-stepping into town one day in 1938 and made him run for his life.

For years I treasured those toy soldiers, and almost wept with the pain of irremediable loss, having passed them to my own son when he turned seven, only to find them again one day lying with their lances broken, the catapult collapsed, and their hand-painted bellicose looks almost completely effaced. But how could I blame him? Our associations are not the same. Abandoned in a heap beside the more perfect, schematically conceived Playmobil knights (likewise of German fabrication), gathering dust, I might have shrugged off the sorry sight, but for a stray eyebrow and the lone pupil of a painted eye that peered out of a broken plastic husk.

4

A Gift

A LITTLE PACKAGE ARRIVED IN THIS MORNING'S MAIL that gave me a good deal of delight. It was sent by a corporate lawyer, plump and buttoned-down, very proper-looking in a three-piece suit, who'd approached me to chat over wine and nibbles following the fellows' presentations at the Academy the other evening. We'd struck up a friendly conversation after discovering our shared fondness for marzipan and those two little cartoon rascals Max and Moritz. The package contained an English translation of the turn-of-the-century cartoonist Wilhelm Busch's classic compilation of nasty nonsense, popularized in the U.S. as *The Katzenjammer Kids*, as well as a copy of the nineteenth-century educational children's classic, *Struwwelpeter*, the latter translated into English as *Slovenly Peter* by none other than Mark Twain. Hard to fathom Huck Finn's confabulator riding the raft of fantasy transplanted from the muddy Mississippi to the Havel and the Spree. Lawyers here apparently still read other things than statutes and legal briefs. Time is not always money in Berlin, sometimes it just ticks.

I can't say why, but for me *Max und Moritz*, that wicked inked and illustrated compilation, tastes of chocolate-covered marzipan—the bittersweet craving for which I must have kept suspended among disused taste buds until it burst forth again at the back of my tongue in Berlin.

And *Struwwelpeter* still sends chills down my spine. Particularly the cartoon about the disobedient boy who, like myself, wouldn't stop sucking his thumbs. Warned by his mother that if he did not desist, the merciless tailor upstairs would come down with his massive shears and snip them off, he persisted with his nasty habit. And so, of course, it came to pass that the tailor stormed in unannounced, and *snip snip*, left a weeping boy with bleeding thumb-stumps—speak of castration complex!—and drops of blood to stain the last frame. Finicky eater that I once was, how can I ever forget that other cartoon character in the collection, *Suppenkaspar*, the original anorexic, who would not eat his soup, and consequently wilted in frame after frame into an ever thinner stick figure, until he simply ceased to be.

It was as if we'd communed, the lawyer and I, on a very private, practically pornographic plane just this side of propriety, a sedimentary layer of consciousness deeply imbedded in the infantile substrata of the German imagination—in my imagination too, or at least the part of it that's German. It's a kindred zone to the gruesome playing field of Grimms' fairy tales, the prickly delight of which lies precisely in the fact that dreadful things do happen, parents abandon their children and witches covet them for lunch, our fear of which becomes a precious plaything, defanged by the power of make-believe. This fascination with the fearful, I firmly believe, lies at the root of German fantasy.

Max and Moritz were very bad little boys who surely deserved a good dressing down, but their grisly fate immortalized with gusto by Busch—to be clubbed to death and dumped by an irate miller into the grinder and minced into bird feed, their recognizable patterns replicated on the mill floor, only to be pecked away by hungry ducks that waddle off, fattened and content—still makes me wince and choke back a grin.

It's the same German humor-mill that made my father refer to his belly as his "*Backhendlfriedhof*," his fried chicken cemetery, the last resting place of many a Jersey pullet. The same dark Teutonic wit that inspired my step-grandmother Jenny as a disciplinary device to regale and reel us in with tales of Unterkralowitz, an apocryphal camp for naughty children, run by the shadowy pedagogues Frau Pospiszil and her tall, haggard partner Dr. Hagatai, the latter wielding a big whipping stick; the same grim humor that surely must have given the future architects and engineers of the chimneys of Treblinka a chuckle in childhood and later as grownups when real-life Hänsels and Gretels went up in a puff of smoke.

This is the bittersweet marzipan-flavored sediment of my imagination, what I taste when I burp in Berlin.

5

Of Sublime Ecstasy and Guttural Disgust: My German Language

*W*HAT IS IT ABOUT THE GERMAN LANGUAGE THAT so moves me? That push and pull of contradictory impulses, that never-ending string of nouns and adjectives in search of a predicate verb to bind meaning, that strange amalgam of superlatives and expletives exuding sublime ecstasy and guttural disgust! German curses and cajoles, belches, farts, and philosophizes with boundless delight, then retreats suddenly, tightening its belt, squelching its own wild urges with the syntax of discipline and restraint. German sentences are chiseled, each a miniature Gothic cathedral, replete with grinning gargoyles, stained glass, and flying buttresses; each a catacomb of neatly stacked bones crowding the unconscious.

How much German infuses every fibril of my being!

Two tongues tugged at my childhood heart and mind, two takes on the world, two flavors of consciousness.

English was the public channel of communication at school and on the street, a peppermint tongue that stung and excited. German, all chocolaty, viscous, and sweet, was the private funnel of intimacy in my first generation German-speaking-Jewish immigrant family. And though I'm a native New Yorker, my emotional grounding is still and always will be in German, the dialect of that tiny city-state of five afloat in the teeming megalopolis.

English meant business, sharpened no. 2 pencils, white shirt and tie; commerce: "I'll trade you a Roger Maris for a Mickey Mantle!"; and diplomacy: "If you don't, I won't be your best friend anymore!"

German coddled, cursed, and cajoled. "*Wir sind jung, die Welt ist offen!*" (We are young, the world is open!) my mother invoked a Socialist marching song from her youth between the World Wars to rally the ranks at reveille and again at bedtime and buck us up when spirits were down. My father fondly referred to us kids as his "Affengesindel" (monkey mob) or "Arschgesichter" (ass faces), depending on our manners and his mood—language the like of which we wouldn't dream of using outside the home. While English called for good behavior, German was a license to relax, in the spirit of father's favorite schoolboy verse:

Salomon der Weise spricht:
Laute Schasse stinken nicht,
Aber jene leisen die unhörbar durch die Hose schleichen,
Mensch, vor denen hüte dich,
Denn die stinken fürchterlich!

(Roughly: Salomon the Wise once said it:
Loud farts smell not, but hear me now.
Those quiet ones that slither through,
Beware of them, I'm telling you.
Hold your nose, or you will dread it!)

The cost of my linguistic split personality was a certain confusion. At times I felt off-kilter, an alien at home plate. There was something perennially out-of-sync in the swing of my baseball bat, as there was, and still is, something not quite kosher about my English, a tendency to over-articulate, "public speak" it, which in the slurred "slanguage" of *Nooyawk* amounted to an accent.

It was the early fifties, and the great cataclysm of World War II was still fresh in everyone's mind, so fresh nobody wanted to be reminded. German was taboo, the tainted tongue of evil. And that a Jew should speak it seemed particularly inimical. Yet despite considerable pressure from relatives and peers, my parents refused to blame the language and stop speaking it. For to excise German would have been to cut out their own tongues and grant the nasty little man with the mustache a second victory.

Years later I found it difficult to get intimate in English. In a college writing workshop, the instructor prodded us to speak and write frankly and openly about our private life, such as it was. With my girlfriend of the moment seated beside me, I put my foot in my mouth. We were discussing the colorful language in one of Henry Miller's *Tropics*, and I awkwardly referred to the sexual organs as the stick and the hole, because my tongue was locked in a pre-adolescent limbo and, believe it or not, the English words penis and vagina were not a part of my vocabulary. I can still feel the sting of the All-American laughter.

★

For me, the big abstractions, like "*Liebe*" (love), "*Traum*" (dream) and "*Tod*" (death), will always resonate in German and somehow fall flat in English. For me the English word "remembrance" has a vaguely vulgar ring, like groping around in the flea market of the mind and subsequently reassembling the cracked and broken bric-a-brac; whereas the German word "*Erinnerung*," (literally a turning inward) raises the conceptual bar, upgrading those haphazard knickknacks into precious antiques.

Sometimes, indeed, I doubt my own identity. Am I myself, or a blatant case of identity theft, a ventriloquist or a ventriloquist's dummy? Are the words I speak my own, or is my subconscious merely taking dictation in a secret code and automatically translating the original German before I wake, superimposing my exhalations with borrowed English meaning? To this day, I often feel like one of those plump, round, hand-painted, Russian, wooden Martryuschka dolls, with German imbedded in my English, Yiddish hidden inside the German, Hebrew pulsing in the Yiddish, and the universal cry of the newborn echoing within.

6

Dietrich Undressed

"Ich hab' noch einen Koffer in Berlin."
(I still have a suitcase in Berlin.)

—Marlene Dietrich

SHE IS LEGS, SHE IS GUTS, SHE IS SEX, AROUSAL, AND restraint. Even in her seventies in the cheesy photo on the faded record jacket of a 33 rpm album prized by my father, the soundtrack over-orchestrated by Burt Bacharach, and skipping, Dietrich's siren song is what men dream of. With a voice like a scratched record, she can compete for effect with any opera diva and still draw a more ecstatic crowd, belting it out for the boys in the backroom, as she did in *Der Blauer Engel* (*The Blue Angel*), the 1930 movie that made her famous:

Ich bin von Kopf bis Fuß auf Liebe eingestellt,
Ich kann halt Liebe nur und sonst garnichts.

(I'm sold on love from head to toe,
Love is all I know and nothing else.)

Reformed femme fatale, vixen turned heroine, eluding the innuendoes of Dr. Goebbels, who sought to make her a Nazi screen star, she ran off and embraced Hollywood, and with it the world—arguably Berlin's greatest export, the Axis Powers' greatest tactical loss, and the Allies' greatest gain after Albert Einstein. And for nostalgic émigrés, like my father, not only did she remain the iconic blond Venus, before Marilyn Monroe and Brigitte Bardot, the idol that primed his portable libido, but also a statuesque German Athena, a veritable Blitzkrieg on two legs to fling back at Hitler. Dietrich did good and made headlines in the process. No other star ever got such good press for changing studios.

And when, in 1984, Austrian actor-director Maximilian Schell sought to shoot a documentary, the highlight of which was to be an exclusive videotaped interview of the famously reclusive star in her Paris apartment in her twilight years, wily Marlene neglected to inform him, until he showed up with the camera crew, that he was free to film everything but her face. She, the original blond bombshell, would remain unseen, a disembodied voice, a teasing absence. But her smoky impression still filled the silver screen, her cigarette-smoking grunt and growl made the movie more memorable than any other Hollywood biopic before or since.

And even faceless and bodiless she continues to posthumously enthrall, her glamorous wardrobe having been acquired by the Berlin Filmmuseum, at Potsdamer Platz, the prize of the collection, like the relics of a saint,[4] the last display you see before filing out, so that the sons of her erstwhile fans can still admire the tight-fitting, fading contour of the myth. Gruff and grinning, teasing and withholding, daring and endearing, the Blue Angel rises again, phoenix-like, to entice posterity with peacock feathers and black garter belt—the sultry soul of Berlin.

★

This afternoon I flung open the laundry room door, intending to do my wash, and was greeted by the sight of the lovely bare long legs of a young woman on staff who shall remain nameless, curled in scant panties on a stool beneath the cover of a blue silk blouse. Looking up, she paused, her face flushed with shame. It took me a blink to unglue my eyes before she retreated to a back room.

---

[4] Speaking of sainthood, the following anecdote is told about another famous Berlin film export, director Billy Wilder, of *Sunset Boulevard* and *Some Like it Hot* fame, who worked for the American occupation force interrogating prisoners. Wilder was lobbied to overlook certain improprieties in the recent past of the actor who had played Jesus in the Oberammergau Passion Play so as to permit him to resume the role again after the War. The man, it seems, had been a notorious Nazi. Whereupon the wily Wilder quipped with his sardonic *Berliner Schnauze*: "Only if they use real nails."

In response to which the Academy's unofficial den mother, Gabi, flashed me a wink. A sassy blonde with bona fide *Berliner Schnauze* (Berlin lip), whom I'd once witnessed in little but her tights changing in the same laundry room, that doubles as a staff locker room, Gabi is no slouch herself. Engaged in ironing Lorelei's slacks, she shrugged: "*Ist doch nur ein Hintere und ein paar Beine!*" (It's nothing but a butt and a pair of legs after all!)

To which I nodded, unconvinced.

Whereupon Gabi waved me off with a gutsy Dietrich grin: "*Ach was!*" (Go on!)

★

And just the other evening I stumbled in late for dinner, a high society occasion hosted by the new American ambassador and his comely brunette wife for visiting stage and screen actor Frank Langella, at which a stunning blond German television star, whose name I can't recall, radiated a blinding golden loveliness, riveting every man's gaze, including mine. I lingered at the dining room door. Then a dark-eyed, dark-haired beauty on the Academy staff, who likewise shall remain nameless, caught sight of me, smiled, shook her head, stormed over in a feigned fury, grabbed hold of my wrist, and led me along, like a bad little boy, a modern day Max or Moritz, to my assigned seat at table, and—Dare I admit it?—I dragged my feet with a sheepish grin, wanting the sweet punishment to last. Langella spoke of impersonating Nixon, Dracula, and other plum parts. The ravishing blonde complained of the competing appeal of reality T.V. and the lack of challenging female roles nowadays. But I was hardly listening, drunk with a lingering delight and still savoring the humiliation of that punishing promenade.

★

It's my mother who led me by the hand across the boulevard of childhood when the red light relented and the green light said: *Geh!* Walk! My mother, whose death, four years gone by now, robbed me of my sleep for a full month, turning everything topsy-turvy, rousing disturbing echoes in the tongue of my begetting, binding me to the frozen ground that took her back, and on which I go slipping and sliding like an unstrung marionette.

Red Light, Green Light, One, Two, Three.

Waiting yesterday for the appearance of the *Ampel-mann*, the spritely little green man locked inside every Berlin traffic light—one of the few surviving relics of the dissolved German Democratic Republic—to usher us safely across time and space, I helped an old woman, somebody else's mother, cross the icy slippery streetcar tracks at Alexanderplatz, her trembling arm in mine.

7

Poultry Epiphany

TODAY CHEF REINOLD TOOK ME INTO THE KITCHEN to show me the ducks he planned to roast for dinner the night of my talk. I'd told him about my mother's parents' poultry stall in the marketplace in Vienna before the War, and of my father's fondness for chicken, how an appreciation of poultry is a part of my heritage. We agreed it had to be roast duck.

Reinold says he converses with his ingredients. He loves to talk to carrots, for instance, and to chat with chives. He hauled down the great crate of eight ducks from a shelf in the massive refrigerator and opened it as one would a treasure chest. There they lay, the little darlings. It's the yellow hew of the skin that makes them luscious, he points out, pinching the flesh, and the fact that the fat, which peels off easily from under the skin, does not resist his caresses, disintegrating easily between thumb and forefinger.

He invites me to take a pinch. Which reminds me of the pinch of my father's Polish cousins twice removed, that painful lobster claw clasp of purported affection that grasped a hunk of child cheek and would not let go until you begged for mercy. "Good enough to eat!" they always winked.

I venture to suggest, and Reinold agrees with a grin, that the cheeks of seasoned statesmen, like those soon to regale us at the upcoming conference on nuclear disarmament, though tender from smiling, are probably too tough to digest.

The ducks, he says, will be filled with orange pulp and rubbed with orange peels, which makes my mouth water.

Reinold leads me on a personal guided tour of the kitchen. We stop to admire his smoker, where he is preparing smoked dover sole, and his oven, his magic caldron, where the ducklings—eight months old, he guessed, nine at the most—will roast on separate shelves, and then lie for a day, tenderizing in their own fat before being re-roasted the night of my presentation. He shows me his knives and the industrial ruby rod he uses to sharpen them. He brings out his stock of balsamic vinegars; we hold out pinkies to taste a drop—a divine harmony of sweet and sour.

He shows me the cod caught in the winter waters of Scandinavia. January, he says, is the optimal moment to fish them out. We put our noses to the fish flesh, and indeed, it does not smell fishy, but wears the perfume of its origin in the salty deep.

He teaches me the German term for the rich red wine we toast with—"*mit Bauch.*" I love the image, a wine with belly, as if each drop embodied Bacchus himself with his own bulging *Backhendlfriedhof*!

He, too, feels an affinity for poultry, Reinold admits over a glass of Burgundy, and proceeds to tell me of the epiphany when he was ten and his mother solemnly instructed him to watch over a duck roasting in the oven, not to let it burn, but not to add water either, for that would dilute its natural juices. And he remembers watching the water evaporating fast, knowing that the birds would burn, but not daring to add water, because his mother had warned him not to—a terrible quandary, the culinary equivalent of finding oneself between a rock and hard place. And, of course, the bird burned, and his mother got mad. And afterwards he vowed never to let such a thing happen again, to understand and master the process to which he has devoted his life.

Twice he emerges from the kitchen to address us at every dinner, first to announce, lips smacking, what we are about to eat, tasting the flavors as he describes them; and then, after the meal, returning to hear the verdict. For Reinold is a true master of the art of the kitchen, ever eager to improve his art.

★

The dinner, the dinner, dear reader, of the dinner I will tell, that Reinold prepared to precede my talk. The menu is now a memory branded on the thin skin of my palate, on my tongue, and buried in my own *Backhendl-freidhof*, where the memory macerates and mummifies.

The table was set in the library beneath the benevolently beaming portrait of the banker Hans Arnhold, the erstwhile owner, a man who clearly enjoyed life and carries himself in the painting with an elegance befitting the splendid villa he built on the lake. What dinners did he preside over here? And what dinners did the later interlopers throw, I wonder?

But salivate, dear readers, at the repast I am about to describe. My words can only do poor justice to Reinold's alchemical wonders. There was pan-roasted *baenschi*, a fish I've never heard of, but which I imagine flitting about under the ice of the lake, served on a bed of marinated *passe-pierre*—a savory seaweed, and the chef's subtle reference to my name: Pierre-Peter—with wild herb salad, the wildness just barely tamed by balsamic vinaigrette. And for the *pièce de résistance*, twice-roasted duck in orange sauce—the ducks I glimpsed the day before—cousins of the wild ducks swimming in the river that runs into the frozen lake—Call me a savage carnivore!—on a bed of Savoy cabbage and sweet potato-parsnip puree. The orange peels shaved onto the crispy duck skin and bits of orange flesh sweetening the stuffing made the bird a culinary metaphor, a fleshy bridge to the sunny south, to where perhaps its soul took flight. And for desert, crème caramel, whipped up as a tribute to my French wife.

You might have thought such an extravaganza of tastes would have muffled the tongue of yours truly when it came time to deliver. Not at all! Primed with a palette of flavors, my tongue rose to the occasion. Eat your words! I'd rather have roast duck.

8

Wurst Lust

"Alles hat ein Ende, nur die Wurst hat zwei."
(Everything comes to an end, only Wurst comes to two.)

—German saying

WHAT IS IT, I WONDER, ABOUT THE GERMAN FONDNESS for the flesh of the pig and the Jewish abhorrence of it? Like lust, revulsion too is a visceral thing fueled by the same hunger, only in reverse, a passion linked to the salivary glands that passes down the gullet to tantalize and taunt the gut. For German-speaking Jewish refugees, like my parents, it was a constant tug of war. My mother would not permit it in our home, but my father had to have his weekly fix.

They and others like them came to a culinary compromise at Bloch and Falk, a short-lived kosher idyll of Wurst founded by Berlin émigrés that briefly thrived and then sadly disappeared, as a consequence of changing demographics, on Thirty-seventh Avenue, near the corner of Seventy-fourth Street, in Jackson Heights, Queens, today's Little Bombay where now Indians and Pakistanis, some of them Sikhs, vie with their conflicting tastes and taboos.

In that Jewish replica of German Wurst-lust, the reprehensible pig-craving was painstakingly and precisely transposed, or rather reformed, into a kosher cow-craving. But even as a boy, I fathomed that, to get the flavors right, or at least to find a fair kosher approximation for pork sausage, some enterprising Jewish butcher armed with a meat grinder and a willing tongue, had at least temporarily to suspend his Semitic aversion and embrace Teutonic taste whole-hog, so to speak, applying a Talmudic rigor to isolate and translate porcine products, and beef them up for a Jewish palate.

How well do I remember the grand opening, with banners unfurled and mountains of open *Brötchen* (sandwiches) stacked tall, free for the picking, stuffed with slabs of sausage and smoked meat of every description, *Teewurst, Krakauer, Kopfkäse, Jägerwurst, Leberwurst.*

From near and far they came, the strongly like-accented refugees of my parents' generation, *Refugln*, as we lovingly called them—which to my childish ear, sounded a lot like *Geflügel*, poultry—they had, after all, flown the coop, dressed to a T in tie and jacket or skirted suits, German from head to toe, save a few recalcitrant curls and the sadness of traumatic loss that never quite muffled their innate exuberance. Waiting patiently on line, with their little native-born progeny in tow, their mouths watered for a licensed taste of the Old Country.

One woman, I recall, got so excited approaching the counter she could not control herself and succumbed to a nervous cough that sounded suspiciously like a dog's bark.

"*Bitte, Lise!* Please control yourself!" her mortified husband looked aghast.

But she couldn't help it, and in any case, nobody but me seemed to notice, each customer consumed by his or her own craving. Was it an involuntary response to the scent of sausage, I wonder, or just a bad case of the hiccups mythologized in memory?

But on Saturdays, when Bloch and Falk was closed, and my father, a man of prodigious appetite, wanted a taste of the real thing, my understanding mother turned a blind eye, and let him take my brother and myself along to Schaller und Weber, the German deli in Manhattan, a kind of culinary brothel in my book, to sample a thick slab of forbidden flesh cut off a fresh hot loaf of *Leberkäse*, still steaming under the knife. Sliced by a bald-headed counterman with gold-capped teeth and a grin straight out of a Georg Grosz drawing, it was the incarnation of what he'd fled. My father savored every bite.

*

Pig images are ubiquitous in Berlin almost every which way you look, a split symbol of delight and disgust. Georg Grosz best epitomized the ambivalence in a searing caricature of an army officer as a uniformed pig on display at a show of his drawings and prints, titled "Korrekt und Anarchisch" (Correct and Anarchic), I caught at the Akademie der Künste. There's an undeniable fondness in his depiction too, a curious intuition that war releases sublimated cannibalistic tendencies, and that we secretly crave the flesh of our foe.

Dear mother of mine, forgive me!

Father's insatiable appetite for the forbidden flesh calls out to me from the hereafter, here and now in Berlin with all the gastric contradictions of totem and taboo, whenever I see *Eisbein* (ham hock) on the menu.

No foodstuff better exemplifies the German craving and the Jewish proscription for me than that quintessential Berlin dish, a veritable mountain of pork, comprising the joint between the tibia/fibula and the metatarsals, the tender, fragrant, fat, and fleshy part of the trotter joining knee and hip, or elbow joint and foot. Classic Berlin *Kneipe* (pub) fare, it's pink cured, poached, or boiled, and served up piping hot with a split pea puree and sauerkraut, or, if you prefer, in the Bavarian variant, grilled to a golden brown crisp.

A positively Neanderthal spectacle on the plate, it's a dish that stirs up mixed emotions when ordered in a restaurant. Befuddlement on the part of foreign tourists—"Did you see what he ordered?!"—who try to imagine just what it is and how in heaven's name it fits on a plate. Utter disgust on the part of avowed vegetarians, for whom it constitutes a blatant, in-your-face affront, the very incarnation of meat. And awe on the part of repressed, cholesterol-conscious carnivores, who themselves would not dare go to such extremes in public to satisfy their lust, secretly considering it a pornographic craving best indulged in private.

The disbelief of my fellow diners is palpable as I dig in. Picture the culinary metaphoric equivalent of highbrow opera buffs compelled to witness a wrestling match. It is indeed a sloppy, slippery task to slice through the blubber of the poached Berlin version, and a carnival strongman challenge to crack the crisp crust of the grilled Bavarian variant, and get at the pink flesh within. Did I say Neanderthal? Medieval might be more precise for the Bavarian version. For the skin sits around the fat and muscle like a suit of armor, and the indiscreet diner is obliged to bludgeon it to get to the meat clinging to the bone. Washed down with a mug of beer, *Eisbein* stirs the heartstrings of old Berliners, who see it as a fleshy mascot, a shrunken head of sorts, and in a certain sense, the poached epitome of Berlin.

★

Which brings us to the porcine nitty-gritty. With all those pig innards ground up and stuffed into intestinal skins, indeed it sometimes seems like Berlin itself is a great fat sausage bursting out of its skin.

At Alexanderplatz, the heart, or rather, the belly of East Berlin, the first thing you see upon emerging from the underground station are the *Grillwalkers*, walking human *Bratwurst* ovens, young men with hot griddles wrapped around their middles, and sausages sizzling before them. But where do they keep their raw ware? Mae West would have had a heyday: Are you glad to see me, or is that a *Bratwurst* in your pocket!?

Let's admit it! So help me Freud, they all look like, well, you know what, hundreds of them severed, sizzling, and sheathed in edible condoms!

It's a grotesque image, I grant you, straight out of the grim humor of *Max und Moritz*. But everything about a Wurst is grotesque, including its prone state, dripping with fat and doused with mustard, its crude position imbedded in a bun, with both ends obscenely protruding.

Ah, hell! Why beat about the bush? Perhaps the German psyche (including its German-Jewish variant) is secretly consumed by a fear of castration and/or penis envy, depending on the sex—which, to assuage—they transfer to the pig, and still by lusty chomping. Circumcision, by extension, a metaphoric ritual cropping, must then be a frightening reminder of this squelched urge that cuts too close for comfort. The unspoken reason perhaps that Hitler was a vegetarian.

9

Walking on Water

*T*ODAY I WENT WALKING ON WATER, A LONGSTANDING
Semitic tradition. I waited till the molecules hardened
to a marble finish, until I saw ducks and dogs, lone skat-
ers and competing teams of husky hockey players, and
even a young mother on skates pushing a baby carriage
before her, skidding across the lake. The first steps were

the most unnerving. Would it hold up under Reinold's rich cooking and all that Wurst? I held my breath and took my first step. And when the ice cap proved dependable, I advanced, albeit gingerly, with mincing steps, farther and farther out into the middle of the lake, admittedly feeling somewhat unsettled by the *glug glug* sound of an underwater current flowing underfoot and thumping with a worrisome insistence against the moorings.

There I was, standing, like my sainted ancestor from Nazareth, next to, not inside, sailboats docked for the winter. Oh ye of little faith! I followed the footsteps other foolhardy ice strollers had made, like walking along the minefield of a frozen war. (Allied bombs with unexploded payloads are still being dug up at East Berlin construction sites and defused by robots.) If the hockey players and the mother with the baby carriage hadn't fallen in yet, I figured, I wouldn't either.

Funny, the physicality of the metaphor of walking on water has seeped into my subconscious, and sticks long after my return to dry ground. And now, as I etch my sentiments across the blue computer screen, the letters look like a crow's eye view of footsteps on ice. The screen holds, as did the lake. I think I'll go walking again tomorrow.

I did it again today. The sheets rang against the metal masts of sailboats stranded in the ice, sounding like distant cowbells in the mist.

A frustrated ice sailor had to get out for lack of wind, and I helped him to propel his racing craft until the breeze picked up, his sails filled, and he skidded off. My eyes cast floaters on the blinding whiteness.

It is difficult to distinguish between the caw of crows and the cry of children. Alone on the ice, ears pricked up for the gurgle of undercurrents, no one would have known if I fell in. There is a peculiar bliss in this, not suicidal, but a taste of the eternal, that were I to drown and die under the ice I might be retrieved eons from now, exhibited in a museum and dubbed the Wannsee Man, a proper vintage match for Nefertiti.

★

Is this walking dream or waking reality? There's no clear line of demarcation and in any case no point pretending any longer. The Berlin I'm in is equally imagined and experienced.

They tore down the Wall more than twenty years ago and I'm not about to conjure up a new one, but invisible walls still stand: the remembered rampart that once divided the German geopolitical reality and consciousness, and still separates the disparate longings of "Ossies" (East Germans) and "Wessies" (West Germans) of my generation; and there's another reinforced concrete parapet going up as we speak, dividing hostile mindsets in the Middle East far from the wintry chill; the latter harkening back to still another wall, longed for and wailed after, the last remnant of a temple of tears.

But this is Berlin, not Jerusalem.

I am seated in my cozy digs on the second floor of the lakeside villa built by Hans Arnhold, a banker of Jewish extraction who decamped with his family in the nick of time, salvaging some of his fortune and reestablishing himself in New York, while his digs were appropriated by the Führer, who passed them on to his Reich Minister of Economic Affairs and later President of the Reichsbank, Walther Fink—I mean *Funk*, a Freudian slip, forgive me—the man in charge of the money.

Sooner or later, we'll have to talk about that precious, insidious, stigmatized legal tender that oils the wheels of commerce and industry, makes clocks tick and hearts beat faster, the mere thought of which makes markets rise and fall, women swoon, and men leap out of windows. It was and still is the hidden manna, whose mythically most astute purveyors and possessors, my gang, remain envied or reviled, depending on your perspective. Even Herr Hitler, who hounded out Herr Arnhold and his ilk, because they had a lot of it and knew how to get more, needed as much of it as he could get his hands on to fuel his fantasies of world domination. So he installed Funk here, in part, I suspect—though I can't prove it—so that the secret might seep into Funk and he absorb his predecessor's wiles and ways of amassing money. Recuperated by the American occupation force, the villa was briefly deployed for high brass rest and rehabilitation, before being turned into the permanent home of the American Academy in Berlin with the permission of Arnhold's heirs, who succumbed to the persuasive talents of the late Richard Holbrooke, President Clinton's first Ambassador to Germany, a firm believer that talks might now replace tanks and erudition supplant armaments.

The Academy is an enchanted crossroads, half fabricated, half real, where the ingredients of a rich ragout meet and meld in a gilded pot. Not a melting pot, but the kind of stew pot they use in France for *pot-au-feu*, a pot that retains the traces of past stews, the charred bits along with the savory traces burnt into the metal. The pot is spiked with a defanged hint of the poisoned past flavoring the mix that makes it all the more delicious.

Here twenty-first-century Berlin society simmers and sizzles, as it did two centuries before at the literary salon of Rahel Varnhagen (née Levin), the active Jewish-born catalyst of German culture, where wayward aristocrats, cultured bankers, diplomats, poets, painters and composers, brooders and babblers, the naive and the cunning, dreamers and doers met to make good chemistry together. Up-and-coming young German Romantic writers, like Clemens Brentano, Achim von Arnim, and Ludwig Tieck, flocked to such soirees to sharpen their tongues against the whetstone of tart Semitic wit, until the tide turned, the young men came of age, and it didn't do to be seen among such un-German riffraff. Whereupon they founded their own *Deutsche Tischgesellschaft* (German Table Society), expressly excluding the participation of their former hosts and hostesses.

Then in the 1920s, fashionable Berlin badly missed the freewheeling ways of the worldly and world-weary, and the salons started up again in villas like this, charmed oases on the edge of the city, where high society let it all hang loose. Till the market crashed and the sledge-hammers of reaction came down again, this time with a savage vengeance, and the party was smothered by the Party, hosts and guests scattered into exile or extinction.

★

This house is haunted. There, I've gone and said it. And now I fear you'll think me daft and distrust my every word.

But lying awake, I have heard a rustling in the hallways late at night. A rustling of ladies' gowns and silken under-things, and the muffled sighs of secret admirers who do their best to shroud their lust, for these beauties are the wives and mistresses of mighty men, and it would not do to be seen making eyes at them in public.

How, I wonder, do the ghost groups get along?

Do the high-strung specters of the original residents and their guests merely ignore, or are they oblivious to the more recent spectral arrivals, the phantoms of the booted men in black, their plain-clothed handlers and lovely blond lady friends?

And do the clumsy interlopers, in turn, mingle in the ghost dance they displaced? (I hear the music, the waltz rhythm pulsing in my bones.)

The shadowy ghouls make graceless dancers, awkwardly clicking their heels, their arms flying out like automatons. While the spirits of their predecessors shuffle about, hovering in a honeyed cloud of longing and regret. If there is fury in their hearts I can't feel it. Only melancholy and a certain disdain.

And over there, across the lake, stands the Liebermann-Villa that belonged to Max Liebermann, the once celebrated, now sadly forgotten, German-Jewish Impressionist painter, who lived, alas, to dispel the rosy impressions that propelled his youthful brushstrokes, and glimpse the grim reality, resigning in disgust from the art academy he had founded that no longer exhibited the work of Jewish artists. "*Ich kann gar nicht so viel fressen, wie ich kotzen möchte*" ("I cannot eat as much as I would like to vomit") he is reported to have said, shortly before dying of a broken heart.

And down the block, in that other, still more opulent villa, the site of the Wannsee Conference—what did Reinhard Heydrich, Adolf Eichmann, and the other distinguished experts on deportation and extermination dine on, I wonder, the fateful night of January 20, 1942, on which they formulated the Final Solution? Goose liver and caviar canapés gobbled up with gusto,

I wager, not a one suffering indigestion, washed down with champagne filched from France's finest cellars.

Do the disowned and the disembodied phantoms shuffling about outside my door fathom the upshot of the words being whispered and the toasts being made across the lake? That even their memories and the memories of their memories are to be uprooted and erased from this place?!

I didn't mean to bring up this subject, not now, not yet. Fantasy got in the way. Forgive me!

10

The Return of the Frog King, or Iron Henry

"On Wednesday, at 3 PM, there will be a security check of the building. In case you are in the building at that time, we kindly ask you to stay in your apartment rooms for the period of the security check, which will take no longer than twenty minutes."
—Request from the Academy

BOMB-SNIFFING DOGS ARE PATROLLING THE CARPETED hallways, closets, and alcoves downstairs in preparation for this evening's conference on nuclear disarmament, hosted by and starring Dr. Henry Kissinger. Security is tight. Dr. Kissinger, I hear, has called off the television journalists. After a moment's hesitation I decide to attend. It's not every day you get to meet Dr. Strangelove in the flesh![5] It's going to be a star-studded extravaganza. Other headliners include former German Chancellor Helmut Schmidt and former German President Richard von Weizsäcker, former U.S. Senator Sam Nunn, former Secretary of State George Schultz, and various other aging German and American political heavies of the Cold War Era. The audience is likewise teeming with international VIPs, ambassadors, ministers, and the like. Chef Reinold tells me he's prepared rack of venison "*von Himmel und Erde*" (literally from heaven and earth style), its gamey flesh stuffed with a mix of crushed apples and

---

[5] Apropos of Dr. Strangelove, a curious footnote. I recently learned from a documentary on Veit Harlan, the notorious director of the Nazi-era anti-Semitic blockbuster film *Jud Süß*, that Harlan's niece married the Jewish-American director Stanley Kubrick. I wonder if Harlan himself lived to attend the wedding.

potatoes, his signature dish, symbolically suited to the occasion. I have a weakness for wild game.

And so they came, aged, stooped, leaning on canes, shuffling on walkers, and rolled in on wheelchairs, the dance of the dinosaurs, the white-haired, hard-of-hearing statesmen of yore, gathered to reflect on the impending threat of nuclear catastrophe in the irresponsible hands of today's rogue nations, some of them erstwhile allies. The place is packed. One of the bomb-sniffing dogs sent in earlier in the day by the German police had, I'm told by an Academy staff member, succumbed to canine temptation and gobbled up her lunch. Dogs will be dogs. Statesmen will be statesmen, ever eloquent, attempting to clean up with words the messes they have made.

Seated in the library off to the left, I crane my neck through the open double doors to catch a glimpse in the living room of Dr. Kissinger, former National Security Advisor and Secretary of State to Richard Nixon, a cartoon character straight from a newspaper satirist's pen, emphatically waving his hands in circles as he speaks, as if conducting an invisible orchestra armed with deadly instruments, rife for spoofing.

Part fairy tale frog king, Iron Henry himself, part Metternich, part Bismarck, part Machiavelli, his deep, gurgling, guttural growl of a voice emanates from the pit of his stomach, so that one has the impression when he speaks that what he says has been pre-recorded, that it isn't him talking, but a ventriloquist, or a simultaneous interpreter, perhaps not even present, dictating the words a la Fritz Lang's Dr. Mabuse, and that what we hear is the badly dubbed soundtrack of a low-budget post-War black-and-white foreign film. The heavy eyebrows only reluctantly press out smiles. Where the megalomania came from, and how he got the ear of the powers that be, remain a mystery. I try to imagine him in early childhood, and later as a youngster with a thick German immigrant accent he never managed to drop in the schoolyards of Washington Heights, imposing his point of view. "It *vass* a homerun, I tell you!" Clearly, from early on, others have been listening, and the voice that emanates from the stomach knows that it is being heard and heeded, and so, speaks not so much to the present, as to posterity.

"'We didn't always agree with each other, but we never lied to each other,'" Dr. Kissinger, a statesman on the political right, quotes his sometime transatlantic partner and nemesis, former German Chancellor Helmut Schmidt, on the political left, the latter nodding awake at the sound of his name, then nodding off again.

Introducing Chancellor Schmidt, the moderator quotes him as once having wryly remarked: "Those with a vision should go see an eye doctor." To which, lifting his droopy eyelids, the disgruntled nonagenarian grumbles back with a grin: "I only said that once." To stay awake, the former Chancellor keeps pulling out a box of snuff, taking a pinch, and sniffing deeply, a nasty nineteenth-century practice adopted to replace his twentieth-century cigarette habit, now a twenty-first-century no-no.

There is bloodshot-eyed George Schultz, former Secretary of Labor, and of the Treasury, under President Nixon, and Secretary of State under President Reagan, Watergate veteran and alleged co-engineer of the ill-fated Iran-Contra Affair—Remember Oliver North?—fretting over humanity's imminent demise.

There is former German President Richard von Weizsäcker, a Christian Democrat, who oversaw the end of the Cold War and German reunification, seated easy chair to wheelchair, with Helmut Schmidt, his old Social Democratic rival.

Former U.S. Senator Sam Nunn, the centrist Democrat from Georgia, is on hand, seated, uncharacteristically, far left, warning in his distinctive southern drawl: "We have a race between cooperation and catastrophe."

And for the grand finale, at the crescendo of a burst of verbal fireworks, Schultz paraphrases Kissinger: "We have stolen fire from the gods and need to learn how to control it before it consumes us."

It was, all in all, a very high-octane evening, a remake of *Fail-Safe* with a hint of *It's a Mad, Mad, Mad, Mad World* for the new millennium, with tour de force performances by an all-star cast of has-been movers and shakers, impressive until the spotlight is switched off, and they limp or are wheeled off-stage and back into memory.

I follow Dr. Kissinger to the men's room, mindful of his oft-quoted bon mot, "Power is the ultimate aphrodisiac," briefly imagining piddling side-by-side. But the unsmiling men in black with microphones in their ears block my way and prevent me from taking his measure.

11

Berlin-*Unbekannt/*
Berlin-Unknown

"There is nothing in this world as invisible as a monument."

—Robert Musil

*I*F THE FAMOUS GERMAN PUZZLE MANUFACTURER Ravensburger—a name that my eye falsely confuses with the notorious women's concentration camp, Ravensbrück, ninety kilometers north of Berlin—had to come up with a several-thousand-piece puzzle representative of Berlin, they'd be hard-pressed to find an appropriate image.

Should the fragmented picture made for patient and assiduous reassembly be a view of the Brandenburg Gate, symbol of the reunified city, or a wintry vista of the Wannsee Conference Center covered with snow?

The rebuilt Reichstag, or a telling ruin like the husk of the Kunsthaus Tacheles—the abandoned department store-turned arts center on Oranienburger Strasse liberated by dissident young East German revelers who named it for the Yiddish notion of "tachlis," or "brass tacks"—already being eyed by realtors for demolition?

Should the puzzle represent the Berlin Wall, 1) under construction, 2) scaled by would-be escapees, some caught in the crosshairs of history, 3) stormed by demonstrators with sledgehammers, 4) that segment covered today with satirical tableaux of internationally recognized graffiti artists and dubbed East Side Gallery, or 5) all of the above?

Or perhaps the most apt picture might be that of an empty lot with at least half of the puzzle pieces missing?

★

No one can fault Berlin for the sin of forgetting. Memory erupts at every turn. Cognizant of its past, the city wears its scars with a certain sullen mix of fatalism and pride, like a one-eyed, limping veteran wears his medals.

One German artist half-seriously suggested that the best way to memorialize the six million would be to blow up the Brandenburg Gate, and a conceptual artist with a likewise black sense of humor recommended a perennial traffic jam on the autobahn. Both ideas were overruled.

In the end, American architect Peter Eisenman won the competition with his somewhat more manageable *Denkmal für die ermordeten Juden Europas* (Memorial to the Murdered Jews of Europe), a kind of modern-day Stonehenge, comprising 2,711 concrete stelae of various sizes arranged in even rows on a sloping plane one block south of the Brandenburg Gate. It is indeed imposing and stirring to behold, especially all white in winter. But memorials, however stark, have a way of melding with the landscape. Children play hide-and-seek, daredevil teens leap from stela to stela, and lovers rendezvous among the rocks. And perhaps it should be so. Beneath a panel of scuffed Plexiglas on which thousands of tourists have trodden, the empty shelves of the underground memorial to Dr. Goebbels's book burnings on Bebelplatz, on Unter den Linden, opposite the steps of Humboldt University, is a telling reminder of past excesses. And the *Stolpersteine* (literally stumbling stones) scattered all over town, those little polished brass plaques buffed by anonymous heels to an eerie shimmer that poke up out of the sidewalk, deliberately cause passersby to trip on the names of those who once lived there and the date of their deportation.

★

The most moving monument is also the least visited. A sign with an arrow in the S-Bahn station stop Grunewald points to Gleis 17 (Track 17).

No commuters ever climb the steps. No conductor ever calls out the stop. The platform is deserted. The track itself is overgrown with weeds. Trees have taken root where once trains ran, giving it a strangely bucolic feel. The only sound you hear nowadays is the twitter of starlets competing with the caw of crows. No trains have pulled out of this track since 1945. Joggers and couples and those out walking their dogs favor the spot for its serenity.

Of all the dates and destinations engraved in the grid of rusty steel on the abandoned platform, my eyes fall on: BERLIN-UNBEKANNT…Berlin to Destination Unknown. The date leaps out at me: 11.7.1942—July 11, 1942, *my* birthday, a decade to the day before I came to be. The date is followed by a statistic: 210 JUDEN (210 Jews). Two hundred and ten travelers took a train to nowhere. They sent back no postcards saying: Wish you were here. They never called. They brought back no souvenirs of the trip. They vanished ten years to the day before I appeared on the seesaw of being and nothingness. I pick up and place a rough lump of gravel as a sort of souvenir to mark their passing, and, selfishly, to insist upon my presence.

★

I finally forced myself to visit the House of the Wann-see Conference, the hothouse of the Final Solution, bicycling over and dashing through the gate just before closing. With its elegant gardens and stately facade, it is the very epitome of opulence. The grounds are decorated with neoclassical sculptures of frolicking fauns, gods, and goddesses. Birds flitter about and the lake gently laps at the shore. The exhibit inside is sobering. Panel after panel recounts the history of racial profiling in theory and practice. There is Hermann Göring's letter authorizing Reinhard Heydrich to organize the conference, Heydrich's polite letters of invitation to the participants, and a copy of all fifteen pages of the conference protocol, with the closing words: "The Conference was concluded with the request of the head of the Security Police and the Security Service to all participants to assure that he receive all necessary assistance in carrying out the 'Lösungsarbeiten'" (those essential tasks involved in the solution).

On the wall their pictures are arranged side-by-side based on the relationships of power. Dapper architects of the Final Solution, they look like apostles of a deadly gospel gathered for a grim last supper. There's the gracious host, Herr Heydrich, head of the Security Police, soon to be assassinated by Czech partisans; Adolf Eichmann, organizer of the deportations, wearing the same officious smirk made famous several decades later at his trial in Tel Aviv; and the sardonic Dr. Roland Freisler, infamous hanging judge of the People's Court, who condemned many a defendant, including the plotters against Hitler's life, to hang by piano wire.

It's late and the last visitors are already filing out. I feel affronted to hear the cheerful chirp of laughter emanating from the stairs. The laughter belongs to the museum personnel just getting off from work, whose faces I cannot see, people who ought to know better! The laughter melds with the chirp of a bird that somehow slipped through the door and is flapping about, trapped in the lobby. Then a guard reaches out and catches it, gently cradling the little creature in the cup of his hands, before releasing it out the door.

I can't help but crack a smile.

12

The Museum
of Things

YESTERDAY I VIEWED THE PACKAGED REMAINS OF
several fallen empires pickled and preserved in the hold
of another. I'm speaking, of course, of the Pergamon,
on Berlin's Museum Island, whose vast holdings are a

monumental commingling of visionary megalomania, imperialist lust, and sheer rapacity.

What impelled Schliemann & Co., the godfathers of modern archeology, to rake the deserts and dusty plains of the Near East in search of portable spoils?

Here on display is the colossal Pergamon Altar, the centerpiece and namesake of the collection, the sky-high stone gateway to an ancient Greek seaport, retrieved piecemeal from the smothering sands of Asia Minor, featuring an epic marble frieze of a battle between the Olympians and the Titans.

Finders keepers, losers weepers. It is clear on whose side the Prussians stand, and as with all spoils, what justification of past and future conquest such monumental finds symbolically confer upon the lieges and their lackeys. The visitor is grateful, of course, profoundly so, to these dogged dreamers who devoted their entire lives to digging up the buried bones and pillars of ancient civilization, and leaving them for us to ogle.

Directly behind the Greek gate looms a Babylonian portal and victory lane, with two-thousand-year-old winged lions perched on the pillars, their buffed ceramic fur glittering, eyes fixed on their virtual prey, like they were ready to pounce and devour the visitor.

This chilling spectacle is followed in the next hall, to the right by a carved facsimile of a cave of the Hittites, and to the left, by a scale model of that mythic redoubt, the Tower of Babel, which the Bible blamed for all our confusion. And in the very next room are selected remnants of the great city built by Gilgamesh himself, the man who traveled back through the tunnel of time to meet Utnapishtim, the only mortal who survived the Great Flood.

The overall effect makes the visitor's head turn. You feel like an inconsequential, albeit privileged, grain of sand, allowed to witness the infinite—no, not the infinite, but Mankind's futile attempt to capture the infinite! It is sobering to think that one day, despite each generation's pretensions of permanence and might, it will all come tumbling down again, as did the Tower of Babel and its modern counterparts, the World Trade Center and the Berlin Wall.

What is a museum, after all, but a great mausoleum, with the names of the latest thieves incised on the fading trace of history?

★

This morning the little white bottle of Odol brand mouthwash with its distinctive swan-like looping neck practically leapt out of the display case at the modest Museum der Dinge (the Museum of Things) in Kreuzberg. The sight of it, my late father's favorite brand, had a visceral effect, sucking me down his remembered throat.

Not all the twenty-five thousand objects amassed on the third floor of this refurbished olfactory—of course I meant *old factory*, another Freudian slip—have such a powerful effect, but each tells its own tale and variously moves the viewer, who brings his own set of associations. Lifting the drab lid of the ordinary, positing kitsch and utility, the functional and the decorative, with a defiant nod at the rubbish heap and a wink at posterity, the museum frames things born in the twentieth century with a reverence ordinarily reserved for precious artworks or artifacts of antiquity.

History is a trail of things left behind, like the pebbles dropped by Hänsel in the fairy tale.

So, on the top shelf of one cabinet a row of battered top hats from the twenties—of the kind my dapper Viennese grandfather, father's father, wore—is coupled by a sly curatorial eye with a row of wistful-looking wooden milliner's female dummy heads—of the kind my Aunt Risa, my mother's sister, used to display her hat samples, before she had to close up shop and hightail it to London. All the lust and longing, posturing and primping of the one-time wearers still haunts the felt and wood.

Other cabinets contain trinkets from the thirties, like radios, "*Volksempfänger*" (People's Receivers) as they were known, and such once sought-after souvenirs as a throw cushion embroidered with Adolf's baleful mustachioed mug, for a cozy afternoon curling up with the Führer, atop a row of tin toy soldiers with arms that niftily flick up in a *Sieg Heil!* salute.

A glass case devoted to utilitarian objects of the immediate post-War era salvaged from bomb craters features various highlights of human ingenuity. Here, for instance, is an empty gas mask husk re-deployed as a milk can; a *Wehrmacht* helmet, shellacked, with a handle bolted on, to serve as a handy chamber pot; and another helmet punctured with the holes of deadly projectiles, recycled as a trivet.

And out of the rubble of destruction springs pure poetry. A hollowed out lump of wood of indecipherable origin and function, painted green and carved into a cow with bulging udder, is inscribed with the verse:

Ich bin Muh Muh,
Die grüne Hoffnungskuh
Es soll in deinem Leben
Auch wieder Butter geben.

(I am Moo-Moo,
The green cow of can-do.
May my wooden udder
Be one day filled with butter.)

It might as well have belonged to an ancient Babylonian, like some broken clay jug on display at the Pergamon across town.

13

Grischa

TO MY FRIEND GRISCHA, A GRAPHIC DESIGNER, WRITER, teacher, and founding trustee of the Museum of Things, Berlin is an object-oriented history lesson. Berliner to the bone, his smile is askew with skepticism and his spectacles are forever slipping from the bridge of his nose.

He himself is the felicitous byproduct of an illicit liaison between a Russian-Jewish commissar in the occupation force on a mission to disseminate Russian culture, with express orders not to fraternize with the locals,[6] at the risk of deportation to Siberia, and a young *Berlinerin*, an illustrator, in the Eastern Sector, liberated in more ways than one. Her mindset had been primed a decade before by the visit to another kind of exhibit.

"We are going to see a show, we will not talk about it when we get there, nor will we talk about it afterwards," her art teacher whispered to her, "but remember what you see, it will be the last time in your life you will ever see real art."

What Grischa's mother saw, and never forgot, was the infamous exhibition of "*Entartete Kunst*" (Degenerate Art), assembled under the aegis of Dr. Joseph Goebbels,

---

[6] I am reminded of a conversation I had in 1973 in a shoe store in Forest Hills, Queens, where my parents were outfitting me for the year I was about to spend as a Fulbright Scholar, studying German fairy tales at the University of Freiburg, in what was then West Germany, which fact my proud mother made sure the salesman knew. Whereupon another customer, an old lady with a kindred accent, felt compelled to interject: "Now don't you *interbreed* with any of them! You know what they did!"

Reich Minister for Public Enlightenment and Propaganda, a hodgepodge of tableaux by Pablo Picasso, Marc Chagall, Max Liebermann, selected German Expressionists and other artistic persona non grata removed from German museums. "Tortured Tapestries-Spiritual Degeneracy-Sick Fantasies-Mentally Unsound Incompetents," is how contemporary posters billed it. "See it for yourself! Be your own judge!" the posters prodded like barkers at a carnival freak show.

Some two million Germans flocked to see the show, nearly three and a half times as many as visited the *Große Deutsche Kunstausstellung* (Great German Art Exhibit) of officially sanctioned Nazi art. There is little doubt which exhibit made more of an impression.

"Berlin," says Grischa, "has always been a place where you could see, you could feel, and you could taste the changes in world politics every day."

His Berlin was the severed Eastern sector of the city, viewed from the West as the blindsided hub of a delusional totalitarian state. But for Grischa and his artist friends, idealists all, not blind adherents to an ideology, the Deutsche Demokratische Republik (DDR) was a social experiment that suddenly dissolved out from under their feet in 1989 when the Wall came tumbling down.

Hoping for reform, not dissolution, they found that their newfound freedom was a double-edged sword.

"Before," Grischa explains, "there was a sense that whatever you did, whatever kind of work, you did it for a purpose, for a common good, to uphold a social structure from which all might benefit. So, in principle, and at least partially, in practice, a solitary writer or artist, or a roofer like Honecker"—head of state from 1976 until 1989, Honecker was originally a roofer by trade—"could and did feel that he was building something bigger than himself."

Grischa compares the embattled position of the DDR to that of the state of Israel, of all places. And, indeed, hearing him describe the mindset, not of the ideologues, but of the idealists, I am reminded of the old sunburnt kibbutznik I met in a citrus grove in the Galilee back in the seventies who held up a grapefruit and crushed it in his bare fist. "*Mah ze?* What is this?" he asked of the dripping juice, and promptly answered: "It's my own sweat!"

Grischa tells a story about the writer and filmmaker, Thomas Brasch, the son of a high-ranking party functionary, a Jewish Communist who returned with his family from exile in London to take part in building a new society. The son saw through the hypocrisies and wrote about what he saw, and consequently spent a year in an East German jail. And when he got out and wanted to emigrate—which he could ordinarily have done without any trouble, since he had never forfeited his British citizenship—First Party Secretary Erich Honecker, a personal friend of his father's, who had known him as a young boy, called him in for a private tête-à-tête.

"You were in prison, weren't you?" asked Honecker.

"Yes," said Brasch.

"Which prison?" asked Honecker, even though he of course knew full well where he had been.

Brasch told him the name of the jail.

"I was imprisoned there, too, under the Nazis," said Honecker. "Oh and by the way," he added, "the rain didn't come through the roof while you were there, did it?"

"No," said Brasch.

"Do you know why?"

Brasch shook his head.

"Because I personally fixed the roof!" said Honecker. "And now you want to leave our home, but who will do what you do, who will replace you?"

Grischa translates: "He wasn't saying: We need you as a troublemaker! Just that, hey, you're a member of the family, we need you to hold up your end."

While all Germans celebrated the fall of the Wall and reunification, and East Germans, of course, celebrated the most, rushing back and forth to feel their newfound freedom, "Only afterwards," says Grischa, "did we fully fathom what we'd lost. That powerful sense of place and purpose, of being engaged in a great experiment."

"What's left?" I ask.

Grischa flashes a wry smile: "A museum of things."

14

Professors of the Pavement

BERLIN CABBIES ARE A BREED APART. RESPECTED authorities on traffic patterns, veritable professors of the pavement, conversant as they are with every backstreet and byway of the once divided, now reunited, metropolis, their nonstop commentary, peppered with plenty of *Berliner Schnautze* (Berlin lip), transforms each ride into a journey, tracing the changing fault lines of history.

Take the driver—call him Willy—who whisked me from Wannsee to Prenzlauer Berg. With the build of a longshoreman, the bounce of a boxer, and the smile of a happy man, he easily swung my belongings, stuffed into two heavy bags, from the pavement to the boot of the taxi.

"I like Russians and Americans," he remarked in halting English, gauging my reaction in the rearview mirror, "but I can't abide the Brits."

"*Warum denn?*" (Why's that?) I replied.

"Russians are generous by nature, Americans by custom," he rattled on in his native tongue, greatly relieved.

"And the English?"

"The English are like turtles, they carry their island around with them wherever they go and never crawl out."

"Wasn't Berlin an island?"

"That depends."

By now I surmised that he hailed from the East.

How, I asked, did he experience *"die Wende,"* the turn of events that lead up to and followed the fall of the Wall.

He paused, looked me in the eye, or rather in the eye of my reflection in the rearview mirror. "You're not English!"

"American."

"The Wall's still there, only now it's made of money instead of cement."

Whereupon he told me his story. He'd always been a driver, first of a bus, then of a taxi, then of a limousine for high-ranking Party functionaries. Made enough to live on. Didn't need any more. And the day he heard the border was opened, he decided to visit the West, just to see what it was like. Rumors spread that the border would only stay open for a few hours, and then slam shut again.

"'You have a child,' his father cautioned when he told him where he was going. 'Don't cut and run!'

"'Where would I run?' he said. 'Everything I love is here.'

"We were nobody's fools," Willy looked up again, lest the American in the rearview mirror think otherwise. "I was born in 1963, in the Sputnik Era. In school the teachers taught us that the Soviet Union had never waged a war of aggression. 'What about Finland?' I asked, I'd read my Stalin. The teacher called my father in.

"'Your son,' she said, 'is spreading subversive ideas.'

"'My son,' Father replied, 'is a true Communist.'

"Father's father, a Red, had been arrested and disappeared in one of the Nazis' first concentration camps. Father was drafted into the *Wehrmacht*, but deserted toward the end, hidden by a peasant woman in her potato cellar."

"Just like in *The Tin Drum*," I said, wondering to myself if he, too, had taken refuge under a skirt.

"Every Berliner has a patch of green somewhere," Willy winked. "When the Wall went up, we lost our lot in the West. Remembering the peasant woman's kindness, Father bought a small plot of land next door to her in Kohlhasenbrück."

"Home of Kleist's Michael Kohlhaas?"

"Could be," Willy shook his head, "I don't care much for fiction. Father loved that parcel of land almost as much as he loved life. He planted asparagus, but they didn't take. Mother never came along—I always suspected it was more than a matter of gardening. But the Wall got in the way. Whenever the old man wanted to 'water his asparagus,' I had to drive him more than sixty-seven kilometers around the bulge of West Berlin to get there.

"Came the *Wende*, I said to Father, a construction engineer by training, 'Let's build a house! You've got the know-how, I've got the muscle!'

"'It's too late,' Father said. The peasant woman had passed away.

"The day he died I found a thick packet with my name on it on the kitchen table, stuffed with the blueprints of a house he'd designed...the house I live in today in Kohlhasenbrück."

Willy left the motor running and insisted on carrying my heavy bags the two flights up. I tipped him generously, by Berlin standards.

"It's too much," he said.

"For the rising price of asparagus," I said, and he smiled.

15

The Publisher

SMILES BREAK LIKE THE WAVES OF A PASSING SAILBOAT over the surface of his canny expression, the white curls of his short beard and close-cropped hair indistinguishable from the curling clouds of soft white smoke rising from the pipe forever clutched between his lips. Puffs of pipe smoke bracket each statement he makes. A landlocked sailor afloat in an ocean of books, he keeps lighting and stoking its bulb, his eyes glowing, ever more demonic. The coffee table between us is covered with an assortment of pipes and all the accoutrements of the pipe smoker, along with a dish of chocolate-covered marzipan squares. The big bay windows behind him face the green expanse of Charlottenburg Park. Every square inch of shelf space is lined with books by authors with familiar names, Benjamin, Hessel, Musil, Roth, calling out like old friends met unexpectedly in transit.

Propped up opposite him in an overstuffed easy chair, one knee slung over the armrest, it's as if I've been sitting here forever reminiscing with Peter, an old friend of the same name, who, but for a decade's difference in age and happenstance, might have been me.

The son of German-Jewish refugees, he was born in London, though his English is halting. His parents, suspect speakers of the language of the enemy, like my own, were interned, like mine, on the Isle of Man at the start of the War, and nevertheless persisted in speaking the forbidden tongue. Almost immediately following armistice, unlike mine, they returned to the place that had sent them packing, where Peter grew up and came of age.

His wry expression is that of an old ship's captain, or rather a pirate, huddling in Hamburg harbor, dreaming of buried treasure, in his case the portable kind, a precious stash of words. Formerly a lector for the venerable old German publisher Rowohlt Verlag, some thirty years ago he left to start his own publishing venture, committed—marketing imperatives notwithstanding—to the kind of short prose bursts of brilliance that once blossomed in Berlin. A dying tradition, its best-known practitioners highlight his slender catalogue, great *flaneurs-causeurs* like Victor Auburtin, Arthur Eloesser, and Franz Hessel—the real-life inspiration for Jules in *Jules and Jim*—and Heinz Knobloch, beloved East Berlin raconteur, recently deceased, the last of the line, all of whom would take a stroll and spin a sentence just for the hell of it, not to get anywhere in particular or to make any grand declaration, but for the pleasure of walking and talking.

A consummate *causeur* himself, Peter loves to tell anecdotes, especially of his late beloved dog Bauschan.

"Quite the '*Frauenjäger*,' a real ladies' man, Bauschan could sniff a female out the window three flights below and grow restive, insistent, like his life depended on it. What an exit! His last act was a mad dash down the stairs to couple with a poodle or a setter, during which he fell and broke his back, became paralyzed, and had to be put to sleep. You can't be truly civilized," Peter opines with a puff, "if you've never had a dog."

"I've never had a dog," I confess.

He gives me a long searching look, pitying, incredulous, ever so slightly contemptuous, till at last he relents with a snort, a second puff of smoke, and a smile: "Then you must have a marzipan!"

16

Alexanderplatz Revisited

*T*HERMOMETER READINGS IN THE LOW TEENS NOT-withstanding, at Alexanderplatz and other prime loca-tions around town, urban mirages have been springing up. Potted palm trees are sprouting out of the cement, ringed by canvas beach chairs, mostly empty and billowing in the chilly wind, a few filled with reclining blondes, sporting skimpy bikinis under unzipped parkas, gazing wistfully at the sky. Alexanderplatz is undergoing a sudden metamorphosis from arctic outpost to tropical beachhead.

Have I missed the punch line of an unspoken joke? Or is this a staged illusion to sprinkle a little Italy, to install a stretch of Balkan beachhead in this northern clime, and so, to tide over Teutonic nerves strained to the max?

Can it be Berlin dropping its pants, cross-culturally speaking, seriously feigning and thereby invoking a sunny disposition? Pale as the prized white asparagus now in season, the minions swarming along the imperial thoroughfare Unter den Linden on the East Side must, I imagine, catch the influence and feel transported to the Dalmatia of their dreams.

★

I was once again scurrying along with the crowd, when, hearing a spine-tingling human howl—it really did rip through the air, raise the hairs on the back of the neck, and send chills down my spine—I looked up to see a body hurdling from the roof of the Park Inn Hotel tower, where Cold War spies once swapped and wiretapped secrets. Jesus, a suicide! I froze in horror and a lurid fascination, until the sound was sucked back into silence, a heretofore unnoticed elastic bungee cord snapped, rebounded, and sent the body bouncing back up, to my profound relief and grudging disappointment. Just a Berlin rite of spring? I looked around, but nobody else's heart seemed to have skipped a beat.

*

Berlin Alexanderplatz, the place, the novel, and the movie it inspired come alive, compressed into thirteen episodes packed into a boxed set of DVDs I borrowed from the Academy library, an episode of which I've been savoring every night along with a square of marzipan after dinner, sometimes watching an episode twice or deliberately skipping nights to stretch the pleasure. For two and a half weeks now I have watched actor Günter Lamprecht's stunning portrayal of the unraveling of the life of that Berlin Everyman, sometime pimp, and lovable murderer, Franz Biberkopf, Alfred Döblin's anti-hero, filtered through the alternately tender and testy, wry and raucous lens of the late Rainer Werner Fassbinder's made-for-TV movie. Biberkopf's doings and his undoing comprise my regular bedtime story. I watched, heard, smelled, and tasted every twist and turn of his big burly hulk. When he loved, I loved. When he raged, I raged. And when he went unhinged at the loss of his beloved Mieze, murdered by a false friend, I too went temporarily unhinged. And now that I've come to the last episode, I'd be ready to watch it all over again from the beginning, the way a child returns again and again to certain picture books that retain the drool of his looking.

*

Franz Biberkopf is back. I spotted him last Sunday, at the Mauerpark, a sprawling expanse of scruffy lawn beside a surviving stretch of the Berlin Wall. Mobbed every weekend, come spring, with locals and tourists, young couples, hippies, punks, and picnicking Turkish families, some come to sift through the junk and find cheap bargains and occasional treasures at the sprawling flea market, some to spray paint a new layer of meaning on this old memento of oppression metamorphosed into a freestanding symbol of freedom—the only place in Berlin where graffiti is allowed—or to drink, smoke, frolic in the grass, pick or be picked up, or just enjoy the sudden explosion of spring after a long, cold winter.

Among the most popular magnets of this weekly happening are the stone steps of an outdoor arena, where an enterprising expat, a New Zealander, I believe, set up a karaoke boom box and mike. Members of the audience, most under twenty, sign up to sing out their hearts in this live Berlin reality take on *American Idol.* The audience responds with cheers and applause. The atmosphere is a mix between the ecstasy of a mini-Woodstock and the intimacy of regulars at a Berlin *Kneipe* (bar). One after another, weekend divas and crooners stride to the mike to, more or less proficiently, mouth the lyrics of a hit tune and mimic the gesticulations of the rocker who made it famous.

The mood was sometimes merry, sometimes downright raucous, depending on the talents of the singer. Then all at once, to everyone's surprise, a big-bellied, broad-shouldered, gray-bearded man of indeterminate age and disheveled appearance, looking like he'd sprung from an old movie, stepped forward, and after a moment's conference with the emcee, launched into

Harald Juhnke's German adaptation of Frank Sinatra's signature song, "My Way."

Stunned at first, the crowd fell silent, not knowing what to make of this unlikely performance. But little by little, won over by his scratchy bass voice and the sincerity of his singing, and by the words that rang painfully true delivered by those blistered lips—

Was ich im Leben tat,
das war bestimmt nicht immer richtig.
Ich nahm, was ich bekam,
und nahm manches nicht so wichtig…

(Whatever in life I've done,
it was, I grant, not always rosy.
I took, same as I gave,
and sometimes, well, just let it go…see)

—the crowd embraced him as the darling of the hour. A fierce determination lit up his eyes. Clearly grounded in experience, his delivery transformed the trite into the transcendent, as, flapping the tails of his tattered raincoat that had, on more than one occasion, clearly doubled as tent and blanket, he raised his arms and poured out his heart—

Wenn ich auch ganz gewiss
mich nicht von Schuld und Schwächen frei seh,
Verzeihen Sie, wenn ich sag: I did it my way…

(And if, as you must know,
I had my share of guilt and folly,
forgive me if I say: I did it my way…)

Whereupon cheers went up among the jaded youth. What began as grudging sympathy swelled into outright admiration, and as he took his final bow, the cheers deepened into a heartfelt, albeit fleeting, adulation. Glowing in the thunderous applause, he paused, peering out at the crowd that would otherwise have shunned him, clearly feeling a flicker of joy, before spinning around and disappearing into the faceless mob.

17

But Where Were the Nazis?

THE POSTER PLASTERED ON EVERY LAMPPOST LOOKED innocuous enough. Red on one side, white on the other, it featured a Playmobil figurine with beady black eyes and a toothbrush mustache, circled and crossed out in red, casting a thin gray shadow, with the slogans BERLIN GEGEN NAZIS (Berlin Against Nazis) above and BLOCKIEREN IST UNSER RECHT (Blocking is Our Right) below.

May 1, May Day, is the traditional workers' holiday, the international Labor Day, celebrated with marches, speeches, and picnics by labor unions and parties on the political Left all over Europe. But Germany's neo-Nazis have sought to capitalize on long-festering resentments. Their May Day march and regularly scheduled clash with an anarchist counter-demonstration had in recent years devolved into a messy Berlin rite, monitored, albeit barely kept under control, by the riot police. This year the clash was to spill over into the peaceful residential neighborhood of Prenzlauer Berg, ostensibly precipitated by an angry demonstration by the Left in the Berlin District of Schöneweide, in front of a *Kneipe* ominously called Zum Henker (The Hangman), a known hangout of skinheads and rightwing extremists.

On most Saturdays, baby carriages and bicycles vie for the right of way. But today the prams and strollers of Prenzlauer Berg were stowed away and the little ones packed off to Oma and Opa. In the two decades since the fall of the Wall, this once rundown East Berlin working-class district turned bohemian hub had evolved into a gentrified nexus of cafés, high-end boutiques, and refurbished pre-War facades, its balconies bedecked with plants and draped with rainbow Gay Pride banners and other insignia of tolerance and prosperity.

Prenzlauer Berg is the last place you'd expect to find any sympathy for the Nazi cause. But hordes of young foreign interlopers and "Wessies" had come flooding in, and rents had risen in the wake of the district's facelift and its rediscovery as a bourgeois bohemian paradise, little by little squeezing out the locals. Taking advantage of their constitutional right to march, the Nazis were hoping to make inroads among the disenchanted "Ossies", many surviving on meager pensions and struggling to make ends meet.

The mood was tense. The bad boys in black were due to descend like locusts upon the neighborhood, flocking by train, car, bus, and motorcycle from the neighboring states of Brandenburg, Mecklenburg-Vorpommern, and beyond. The police had closed down S-Bahn stations in the immediate vicinity to avoid violent clashes and keep the counter-protestors at a safe remove. Placards plastered everywhere warned of the impending onslaught. Many residents either left town for the day or hunkered down, having stocked up with enough supplies to tide them over. Windows were boarded up along the Nazis' planned parade route from S-Bahnhof Bornholmer Strasse to Landsberger Allee.

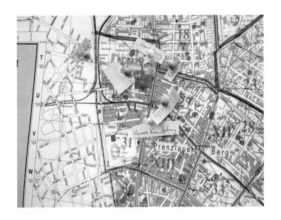

With a mix of indignation and angst, and more than a little curiosity, never having seen a real live Nazi before, I decided to join the barricades of under-thirty-year-olds blocking the Nazis' advance at various intersections. But all I saw was a wall of police.

An ominous threat, they loomed in the distance like a dark impending storm cloud that first made us huddle all the more tightly together, then lifted little by little, and finally fizzled out altogether when word spread that they'd been stopped dead in their tracks. Of the projected horde, a mere six hundred or so reportedly trickled into the neighborhood. But I never set eyes on a single Nazi, and sadly regret it, as I would have liked to have been able to report upon their manner and appearance and maybe even interview one.

The crowd I'd joined had staked out a position under the tracks at the S-Bahnhof Schönhauser Allee, directly behind a line of helmeted, shield-wielding, grim masked riot police, themselves, in turn, backed up by a wall of armored police vans ringed in a semi-circle defense formation like Conestoga wagons in the Wild West, everyone waiting in vain. Stopped allegedly by some two thousand protestors at the corner of Wisbyer Strasse, and another thousand at Wichertstrasse, our bêtes noires were obliged to do an about-face and retreat back the way they came, having managed to march a mere nine hundred meters before calling it a day.

Though pleased that the blockades had held them

off, I was envious of a friend who said he saw some barking like a pack of coyotes in a subway station, surrounded by police, and at least had the satisfaction of jeering and hurling insults.

But their threatened appearance served as a magnet to draw together a most congenial crowd, some armed with banners, like BERLIN BLEIBT BUND, SCHEISSE BLEIBT BRAUN! (Roughly: Berlin Remains Red, Shit Stays Brown!), clasping green balloons marked NAZIS RAUS! (Nazis Out!), and cheerfully popping beer bottle tops, determined not to let the absence of the enemy detract from a chance to have a good time.

I talked with two protesters, a young man in his twenties with shoulder-length brown hair, and his bespectacled, blond-haired friend, both well-mannered, well-spoken members of a youth group affiliated with *Die Linke* (The Left), the recently established political party comprising the left wing of the SPD (the Social Democrats) and the former Communists.

"Why are you here?" I asked.

The brown-haired one hailed from a village in Brandenburg where widespread unemployment and low wages for the lucky few who had work fostered a sense of hopelessness for the future. While he sympathized with the despair of his peers, who came of age in a world that seemed to have "left them behind like the broken parts of an obsolete social machine," he condemned their tendency to lash out against imagined enemies. "I need to remind them that the enemy isn't wearing a burnoose or a burqa, but a three-piece suit."

"Are the Nazis a real threat?" I asked.

"Only if we let them be."

His Berlin-born bespectacled buddy interrupted with a pained pinch of the eyes: "The threat is real until we face it in ourselves and root it out!" He recently learned that, contrary to family legend, his father's father was not the valiant soldier fallen on the Russian Front, as he'd been given to believe as a boy, but a member of the Waffen SS, the killer elite, arrested and executed by the Poles. "I had always treasured his memory before," he said, "and now it's like a cancer I carry in me."

"The press depicts us as young hotheads," the brown-haired one added. "It's good to have an old timer like you"—I winced at the designation—"and a foreigner to boot, join the blockade."

★

On the S-Bahn ride home from the blockade I witnessed an unsettling interaction between competing panhandlers. A wiry, determined homeless man, not much older than the two I'd talked to, peddling a newspaper by and about the homeless, but who couldn't seem to sell a single copy—something about him repelled all sympathy—grew suddenly incensed at the incursion on his perceived turf by a pair of dark-eyed, dark-haired musicians, a fiddler and a guitarist, presumably Roma, who climbed aboard at the next stop and immediately filled the train with their merriment, drowning out his dour harangue. Speechless he listened, literally grinding his teeth in rage—you could almost see the smoke rise out of his ears—until the fiddler doffed and passed his hat, and people responded with a tinkle of coins. Whereupon, unable to contain his fury any longer, the homeless man stamped over and half-howled, half-hissed, his throat hoarse from hawking papers: *"Auschwitz öffnet die Toren für Euch!"* (Auschwitz opens its gates for you!) I could not at first believe my ears and eyes, watching him sneering in the wake of his words, savoring the bile that mounted his esophagus and poisoned his lips. But the merry musicians either missed or ignored the message and went right on playing.

18

Spring Reawakening

T HIS MORNING I FOUND THE FOLLOWING TONGUE-IN-
cheek message in my inbox:

PLEASE TAKE NOTICE

Please be aware that because of the weather
conditions it is NOT RECOMMENDED ANYMORE to

walk on the ice of Lake Wannsee or any other lake (unless you consider yourself to be a great northern diver).

Impossible to describe the beauty of yesterday's sunset over the lake glimpsed at the dinner table out the corner of my suddenly squinting eyes. So much was I stirred by the spectacle I watched unfurl that the business of seeing took sensual precedence over the business of sustenance, and I don't remember what I ate. It started as a cool pink, a faint blush on the horizon, of the sort that surely impressed Liebermann's brush. But the water kept begging for more, its ripples greedily drinking and reflecting every shade of crimson from above; now in a dapple of pink, like an apricot when it's just ripe; now in streaks of cranberry; now in a wash of rouge spread haphazardly, like a little girl's makeshift endeavor to mimic her mother's more experienced application of make-up, or an aging tart's pathetic attempt to reclaim her lost allures; now in broad ruby stripes; now in blood-red swathes, as if the sky itself were an assassin, having murdered the sun; now in bands of deep purple fading to black, infused to the last with the memory of red.

Such a sudden burst of color can make a man delirious in Berlin. I meant to rush to my room to grab my camera and capture the impression, but riveted to the spot, I just let it strike my eyes.

★

Of all the odd birds that converge upon and brood in Berlin, two most embody the spirit of the city, albeit for seemingly antithetical reasons: the *Rabe* (raven) and the *Mauersegler* (black martin or swift), the former reviled, the latter revered. The wily raven, in Norse lore known as the bird of wisdom, once proudly perched on the shoulders of Odin, the king of the gods, has fallen on hard times, demoted by Christianity into the bird of ill omen.—Remember Hitchcock's villainous assailants and Poe's plaintive refrain!—It tends nowadays to favor graveyards and empty lots. Still one can't help but admire its pluck.

I saw one black-winged curmudgeon go hopping, unflappable, along the track at the S-Bahn Station at Wannsee, with a proprietary step, like it owned the line, daring any other living creature to displace it. A

homebody, the raven sticks around all winter, scream-
ing its seeming displeasure, while scavenging for slim
pickings. As children we were dubbed by our parents
"*böse Raben*" (bad ravens) whenever we disobeyed, so I
have always harbored a certain secret fondness for its
stubborn streak.

The *Mauersegler* (Apus apus) couldn't be more different. A winged acrobat, similar to, but not to be confused
with, the common swallow, it sleeps, mates, and carries
out all of life's essential acts in midair, flapping for days,
weeks, months on end, apparently traveling some ten
thousand kilometers from its winter holiday in Africa to
niches and sheltered crevices in walls, never descending
to level ground.

A sometime resident of the former GDR, where it
nested in large numbers and was greatly prized, the bird
came to symbolize a longing for transcendence. Its very
name, *Mauersegler*, literally "wall sailor," evoked a challenge to manmade limitations that has survived the fall
of the Wall. The bird could nest anywhere from Mada-
gascar to Milan, but chooses to return to Berlin.

It might have been a Mauersegler singing at sunset
on the lake. At a concert at the Academy on the first
warm evening in spring, someone opened a window,

and that itinerant chirp answered the wail of the cello and the whine of the violin, and for an instant everyone paused to listen to its astounding solo as the sun set over the lake, its song echoing harmonies and dissonances, reflecting jagged edges, runs in stockings, streaks in the sky, heartbreak and ecstasy, luck good and bad, and the nebulous territory in between.

★

Like the birds and the bees, they too were out and about, and like strange exotic flowers they sprouted suddenly that first warm weekend of spring among the sunset stream of strollers, tourists and transients, couples, families and loners thronging Oranienburg Strasse, just down the block from the glistening arabesque facade of the reconstructed gold-domed New Synagogue. Posing tall and slender, almost ethereal, with a blank Pre-Raphaelite stare, like fashion models on which to drape your lust, their make-up and dress no less extravagant than that of the golden girls who make it into *Vogue*, and like long-necked swans, they lingered immobile or floated by, inviting stares.

I surreptitiously pulled out my Olympus to snap

the picture of one blond vision of loveliness straight out of the twenties, at the busy corner of Oranienburg and Rosenthaler Strasse. But no sooner did I snap than the lovely creature shot forward with a hiss—swans, I'm told, can get nasty—and to my profound embarrassment, grabbed hold of the strap of my camera.

"Oh, no," I lied, "I'm only interested in the Art Deco architecture of the doorway."

Half sneering, half grinning, she reached out and clasped my equipment, compelling me to show her the shot, in which her figure filled the frame.

"Architecture, my ass!" she snickered, and made me delete her image.

★

All winter long passersby enjoyed the idyllic spectacle of fathers and sons sledding down snow-covered slopes on the street-side of the Park am Friedrichshain, the city's oldest public park. Little does it seem to matter that these hills are not of natural origin, but, rather, comprise the rubble heap of war ploughed under and piled high over reinforced concrete air raid bunkers too resilient to explode. That was then, this is now.

Kaizers, la banda que rompe con los

POR ALLAN KOZINN

Las circunstancias difícilmente podrían ser más extrañas: un sexteto noruego de rock alternativo que sólo canta en n...

eran ado...
el sud...

spiado?

No son sólo los
gobiernos los que
stán al acecho.

And on the pathways of the park, in the euphoria of a long-anticipated spring, a cottony white efflorescence falls from the trees in certain lonesome spots. I saw a boy pick up a fistful and fling it like a dissolving snowball at a giggling girl.

"What is it?" I asked another passerby, bedazzled by the spectacle.

"*Pappeln*," he said.

Poplars, or cottonwood trees, spread their seeds in pods surrounded by a willowy white substance that looks and feels like cotton underfoot, thus the name, and from a distance it glistens like snow. It is as if, accustomed to being buried in drifts, the city felt naked without a white coat.

19

In Search of Lost Shadows

*I*T WAS A SUNNY SATURDAY, A WELCOME RELIEF AFTER a long gray winter. I drove with a friend out to Kunersdorf, a sleepy village an hour east of Berlin's urban sprawl, though infinitely farther in heartfelt time and space, where the scattered ruins of disaffected factories give way to wide open fields.

A castle once stood here belonging to a certain Count von Itzenplitz, a name with a comic fairy tale ring, like Rumpelstilzchen, Rapunzel, and Rotkäppchen (Red Riding Hood). Leveled by the winds of war, the erstwhile structure's phantomlike presence is still implied by the oddly shaped gap between the trees and the duck pond. It was here, while tending the von Itzenplitz's garden and herbarium, that the poet and botanist Adelbert von Chamisso (1781-1838), a French émigré who fled Berlin to escape conflicting loyalties and the warring forces of his day, composed a fairy tale about a man who barters his shadow to the devil for a bottomless sack of gold, and is thereafter doomed to wander shadowless through life.

Certain works erupt as naked emanations of the soul, bursts of pain transmuted directly into poetry. Such was the case with Chamisso's *Peter Schlemihls wundersame Geschichte*, a text that became an international bestseller almost immediately upon its appearance in 1814 (and which I retranslated into English some years ago). The devil's come-on at a garden party near the beginning of the tale is one of those unforgettable lines in literature that leap off the page and leave you speechless:

> For the short while during which I enjoyed the pleasure of your proximity, I was struck several times—please permit me to remark upon it—with inexpressible admiration for the lovely, lovely shadow you cast, that shadow you fling to the ground with a certain noble disdain and without the least notice, that lovely shadow lying even now at your feet. I wonder if you might possibly consider parting with it—I mean, selling it to me.

Now the absence of a shadow may well go unnoticed in the dead of a sunless Berlin winter, but in Brandenburg when the buds begin to burst it's a different story.

We had come, Beatrix Langner, Chamisso's biographer, and I, his latter day English amanuensis, to help found a Chamisso Society. And that we did with a proper charter complete with clauses and sub-clauses that Beatrix, the Society's president-designate, had expertly drafted, and which all present first debated point for point, in proper German fashion, and then finally signed, feting the occasion with a swig of white wine and a bite of *Schmalzbrot*, pumpernickel smeared with lard.

In the whimsy of the moment everything took on the feel of a fairy tale, including our names, shades of Beatrix Potter and Peter Rabbit. Among our fellow co-founders was an old white sheepdog, a shaggy throw rug come alive, that wagged its tail and alternately barked and growled to express assent and dissent, and its mistresses, the three aging residents of the *Musenhof*, the muses' lodge, where the signing took place.

Fairy tale characters in their own right, these three ladies were a cross between Goldilocks's three bears, Snow White's seven dwarves, and Sleeping Beauty's fairy godmothers. The most congenial of the three, who smiled and seldom made a sound, except to clear her throat from a lingering winter cold, was husky-voiced and big-boned, looking like she could hold up a house, or build one from scratch. The second, buck-toothed and bespectacled, was the bookkeeper of the bunch. Bookkeeping is an underappreciated but essential skill, in fairy tales as in life. The third, clearly the ringleader, wore a motorcycle leather jacket, like Marlon Brando in *The Wild One*, and a hard-as-nails look that could kill if you crossed her. A rare combination of the ethereal and the sturdy, the precious and the practical, together they somehow managed to transform a broken-down cottage on the grounds of a phantom castle in an economically depressed pocket of Brandenburg into a museum, publishing house, and cultural center.

And while the experience was hardly on the order of the signing of the Magna Carta or the Declaration of Independence, all present felt a certain satisfaction at having had a hand in creating a safe haven for lost shadows.

★

The elusive sun played peekaboo, leaping forth and disappearing again behind a gray cloud cover back in Berlin, Sunday morning, as I headed out to Kreuzberg to complete my pilgrimage.

The poet Chamisso winks and whispers in perpetuity from a memorial plaque at Friedrichstrasse 235, at the site of his last residence (the house itself was flattened by an Allied bombing raid and replaced by a nondescript high-rise):

> I am a Frenchman in Germany and a German in France; a Catholic among the Protestants, Protestant among the Catholics; a philosopher

among the religious, [...], a mundane among the savants, and a pedant to the mundane; Jacobin among the aristocrats, and to the democrats a nobleman [...] Nowhere am I at home [...]!

The neighborhood today is no less cosmopolitan. Turkish immigrants predominate at the far end of Friedrichstrasse, near the U-Bahn station stop Hallesches Tor.

The crowd was loudly and joyously celebrating the end of a long winter, with families and friends gathered in great numbers to grill lamb, play ball, dance and laugh, the men among the men, the women among the women, the children among the children. The cemetery itself, actually a conjoined cluster of several cemeteries: the *Dreifaltigkeits* (Trinity), the Jerusalem, and the Bethlehem, seemed almost out of place beside such messy merriment. Making my way among the revelers, I had the strange sense of passing through a parallel universe, like a ghost among the living.

In the Trinity enclave I stopped to pay my respects to the composer Felix Mendelssohn Bartholdy and the salon hostess Rahel Varnhagen von Ense, the literary muse of the Romantics and a close friend to Chamisso.

"Good people," Rahel gaily greets in perpetuity, holding court from underground, her words inscribed in stone, "if something good should happen to humanity, then in your happiness, also remember mine."

I dropped a white pebble, Hänsel-style, beside her tombstone. It's an ancient Jewish ritual, so that graves not be forgotten in the wilderness. I had pebbles in my pocket for all my friends, regardless of faith.

A pebble for Rahel's fellow patroness of the arts, Henriette Herz, in the neighboring enclave of the Jerusalem Cemetery.

A pebble for the restless raconteur, E. T. A. Hoffmann, resting in peace several rows to the right.

I kept my last pebble for Chamisso.

"*Wo liegt Chamisso?*" Where does Chamisso lie?, I inquired of two men who may or may not have been gravediggers, and looked like they had leapt out of a painting by Peter Brueghel, carousing on the rooftop of a dilapidated memorial chapel, taking potshots with pebbles at the beer bottles they'd emptied. At first confused, and then convinced, as I only fathomed after the fact, that I was asking after the "*Mist*," the refuse, their chuckles swelled into guffaws of laughter, as they pointed in the direction of an overflowing garbage bin.

The only other living soul in sight, a black crow I encountered along the way, intently chewing on the carcass of a rat, could not be bothered to give directions.

But it was a nearsighted rabbit out of *Alice in Wonderland* that led me to the spot. Hopping straight into a stone wall, it ruffled its bruised nostrils and wrinkled whiskers, wiggled its ears, and pivoted suddenly to the left, toward a towering pine and a knotty conifer, at the shaded roots of which, before a tilted tombstone, it pounced on a dried-out bouquet of red poppies.

The resident naturalist on a scientific expedition launched in 1820, sponsored by the Russian Count Nikolai Romanzoff, that landed on the Pacific coast of America, Chamisso named the California poppy (the state's official flower) *Eschscholtzia californica* for the ship's doctor, Johann Friedrich Eschscholtz, who, thereafter, returned the favor, albeit with a certain irony, naming a weed, the silvery bush shrub, *Lupinus chamissonis*, in his honor.

Chamisso would, I'm quite sure, have been pleased to know that a friend from the future was directed to his last resting place by a nearsighted rabbit and a wilted poppy.

★

The sun was setting and my shadow shrinking fast. I followed the path of my pebbles back to the living. The revelers had dispersed, but on my way to the U-Bahn station stop Hallesches Tor I stumbled on an astounding natural phenomenon.

Two conjoined ladybugs were scurrying along the pathway. They looked in the fading light at first like a bickering old married couple, at second glance like a pair of inseparable young lovers, and finally like an insect shadowboxing with itself. Over pebble and weed, dirt and rubble, and up the cemetery wall they scampered in their frenzy, their rapture, or trying to break free. I couldn't tell for sure if I was witnessing a sad domestic melodrama or a lurid entomological love story. Now they crawled over a dead leaf, now they paused, cast worried looks about, no doubt aware of the giant eying them, and scurried on.

And then it dawned on me. Could they/it possibly be a natural anomaly, conjoined Siamese ladybug twins? And might I be the first inadvertent naturalist to report on this freak phenomenon? I reached for my pen and my Moleskine pocket notebook and scribbled the name *Coccinella Chamissonis Gemini*, herewith recorded in Chamisso's honor, but when I looked up again my subject was gone.

20

Recalibrating Time and Space

ONCE UPON A TIME, AND SEEMINGLY FOREVER, IT STOOD
fourteen feet high, spanned twenty-eight miles, and was
Germany's and Europe's ultimate divide. On its western

side, it was splattered with spray-painted expletives, imprecations (KILL FEAR!), recommendations (HANG LOOSE!), pronouncements of love and doom, and sometimes inspired frescoes and artistic installations—one young woman having gone so far as to create a living room environment complete with TV, wall hangings, and a sofa-bed, where she lived for several weeks until the authorities turned her out. On either side stood men in various shades of green and gray, watching and waiting.

★

Times have changed. And now that the Brandenburg Gate is open for foot traffic and a line of bricks runs like a scar along the blacktop down the block from Checkpoint Charlie, where the Wall once loomed, Berlin's sense of space has changed too.

At the BrotFabrik, an art film house in a former bread factory building in Prenzlauer Berg—How was their whole grain bread, I wonder?—I attended the premiere of a rediscovered documentary previously thought to have been lost, one of the last movies produced by DEFA, the erstwhile state-subsidized studio of the GDR. Originally released in 1990, and directed by Gerd Kroske, *La Villette* documents an exhibition organized shortly after Germany's reunification, in which young East Berlin artists—many in the audience now, twenty years hence—showed their work at La Villette in the vast hall in the grid iron guts of the old Paris slaughterhouse district.

Among the movie's subjects is an older painter, Jürgen Böttcher, aka Strawalde, first filmed in his cramped claustrophobic studio in East Berlin, where he shows mostly small cramped canvases, mock-offs of Cezanne and Picasso. The camera catches up with him again in the vast hall in Paris setting up his exhibition space, little by little unraveling his work and his spirit, like a jinni let out of a bottle. Offered a massive blank canvas, he first dances around it, like a dog staking out his territory, then lets loose with spurts of black paint, haphazard splotches, so it seems, till, little by little, they evolve into a labyrinth, to which he sparingly adds touches of color, first red, then blue, leaving corridors of white. "White lets it breathe," he cheerfully chirps with the pathos of a caged canary suddenly let loose. Whereupon, dancing a jig of joy, he starts singing as he paints. It is the song and dance of a spirit set free.

Time matters deeply at this rare moment caught on film, not the shackled Capitalist notion of time as money, but the explosive Einsteinian notion of time as a function of exploding matter and energy unleashed. In this reborn Berlin they re-count time (and recalibrate space) backwards from a new beginning, from the fall of the Wall. Time matters because space matters. Time and space have been released and refuse to be contained. But there is a price to pay.

The movie concludes with its most telling segment, capturing the audacity of a latter-day Wilhelm Busch, an outrageous young cartoonist who all of a sudden applies paint directly to the clear face of a black and white T.V. midway through the screening of a propagandistic idealized aerial view of the former German Democratic Republic, its hamlets, highways, fields and factories, with a grandiose soundtrack by Beethoven, Symphony no. 3, I think, setting the mood. The cartoonist first divides the screen into cell-like segments, like a beehive, which I imagine to be the end of the movie, until he brazenly, mischievously, marks each segment with a sticker price, sometimes in Deutschmarks, sometimes in dollars, the lingering moral left to the viewer as the closing image.

21

The Phantom Flash

FOR YEARS I'D DREADED THE PHANTOM FLASH ON FRENCH autoroutes and Italian autostrade of German headlights blinking in my rearview mirror, warning that I, in my rickety Renault 5 or puny Peugeot 205, had better move off to the right to make room, or be mowed down by a

Blitz on wheels. And every time, heart squirming with fury and frustration, cursing under my breath, I ceded the right of way to a sleek Mercedes or a Porsche polished to an eerie shimmer, whizzing past me practically at the speed of light.

I was driving up to the Baltic Coast for a weekend escape, and as soon as I left Berlin's city limits an impish urge took hold and I lost all control. One moment I was my old meek self, an obedient drone at the wheel, and the next moment I had metamorphosed into a comic book superhero, a kind of Iron Man on wheels—Call me the Phantom Flash!—the shiny black metal body of my rented Mercedes enveloped my flesh and blood body in a sleek suit of armor, a perfect fit; encapsulated by headlights, my eyes spit fire and the rumbling engine tapped the secret longing in my heart.

Gently pressing the accelerator, I hardly felt the pistons pop and the motor surge as the speedometer rose from 130 to 160 to 180, and grazed 200 kilometers per hour, all the paltry laggards, the Hyundais, Hondas, Skodas, and VW Beetles meekly scurrying to the side to make way for my superior engineering. I admit it, all that horsepower went to my head. Diesel fuel rushing like a triple espresso through my metal veins, I was the sovereign of my destiny, the king of the road. Heaven help any puttering peon who refused to bow to my will.

And at that moment I fathomed what it meant to drive in Deutschland. That the autobahn, the super-highway with its absence of speed limits, was the incarnation of Siegfried's bravado. That that ribbon of asphalt plastered over the landscape tearing into the horizon was the last hurrah of German Wanderlust, all that was left of the Teutonic dream of grandeur, of Charlemagne, Frederick the Great, Bismarck, Wagner, and, yes, Hitler, too, flattened out and funneled into a sublimated hormonal rush that could only still be indulged at the wheel of a speeding car.

And as the engine revved effortlessly and the world sped by, reality compressed into the little rectangle of my rearview mirror, nothing else mattered, nothing but the rush of speed and the road ahead.

★

Then it happened after months of excess. The engine stalled. The guts gave way. And all the stuffing of the sausage I'd become spewed forth. All night long I slept fitfully in between epic spasms of heaving. Metaphors are rife in the early morning light. They spew out like ghosts on the battlefield of the id. I tossed and turned in semi-delirium, imagining all kinds of crazy connections, feeling my way back into the mad fit that grabbed hold of this country and this city twice over, first when it retched out its guts, flushing out a segment of the population, and then, after the War, when what was left was divided into two opposing heaps.

★

Peter the Eater exploded. The story is sad to tell. He ate so much he became a walking sausage until he *platzed*. And on his tombstone the tragic words are inscribed: He took so much in, he gave out.

22

Protected

*I*T WAS MY LAST NIGHT IN THE LAVISH VILLA ON THE LAKE
in Berlin-Wannsee where I had comfortably holed up

for the winter. A noted Indian economist was scheduled to lecture on the underlying causes of the global financial crisis and its effects on the developing world. Call me an escapist, but I was not inclined to listen to the sad statistics. The world's affairs would muddle on without me, I thought, intending to grab a quick bite and slip off unnoticed to attend to my packing.

Such dinners were always a festive affair, the guest list sprinkled with Berlin society. My tablemate to the left, the wife of the German theologian seated beside the Indian economist, was a tall, stately woman of late middle age with prominent cheekbones, Prussian blue eyes, and tightly braided, blond hair, who wore her years like a string of pearls. Straight-backed, head held high, as if she were not seated at table, but rather astride a saddle, ears pricked for the sound of a hunting horn, she had what in former times would have been called an aristocratic bearing.

Socially maladroit and constitutionally incapable of making small talk, a tendency further aggravated by chronic insomnia, I either clam up on such occasions or put my foot in my mouth.

Prodding myself to say something before taking up knife and fork to dispatch the appetizer, two luscious-looking, seared sea scallops on a bed of wilted seaweed, I wished her, "*Bon appétit!*"

"*Gesegnete Mahlzeit!*" Blessed meal, she replied.

"Bless the chef!" I countered, immediately regretting the flippancy of my ill-considered response. "Please forgive me, but I'm not a believer."

She smiled to make clear that she took no offense. "Religion is a personal matter. My faith," she affirmed, "makes me feel *beschützt*" (protected).

A striking choice of words, I thought, while savoring the flavor and firmness of the first scallop. "I myself altogether lack the foundation of faith," I confessed. "Given my family history, feeling protected is simply not in the cards."

She seemed concerned, sympathetic, as though suddenly fathoming that I was missing a middle finger.

"I'm the child of refugees," I said to set the record straight.

"Oh?"

I might have changed the subject but I chose not to. With me it's a compulsion, a need to lay my cards on the table.

"My father's departure from his native Vienna was..." I searched for the appropriate adjective, "precipitous."

"Precipitous?"

"Involuntary," I clarified.

"I see."

Decorum should have compelled me to change the subject. But impatiently lapping up the second scallop whole, my tongue rattled on.

"Huddled, to hide his prominent nose, in the side-car of a motorcycle with a swastika flapping in the wind, he was driven by an accommodating member of a motorcycle gang, who agreed, for a fee, to drop him off at sundown at a wooded stretch of the border with Czechoslovakia. And when, at the sound of what he took for a gunshot—but was, in fact, an engine backfire—they suddenly stopped, convinced his time was up, my father held his breath as the motorcyclist dismounted, only to return moments later with a bleeding hare he'd run over, knocked its head against the fender, and asked my father to be so kind as to hold it for him. Fresh meat being scarce, he meant to have it for his dinner."

The arrival of the entrée, rack of venison prepared "*von Himmel und Erde*" (heaven and earth) style, i.e. stuffed with a puree of mashed apples and potatoes, came as a welcome point of punctuation.

She eyed me in between bites with an intense, but

not unfriendly, gaze, as if, I thought, considering a rare wildflower, which aggravated my malaise.

To smooth the way for my escape, I let slip that I was leaving early the next morning for a trip to Poznań, Poland, and so, unfortunately, would have to skip dessert and miss the lecture, to pack.

"To *Posen*?!" she burst out, employing the old German name of the region and city ceded to Prussia following the Congress of Vienna and reclaimed by the Polish in the wake of World War II; promptly correcting herself: "*Poznań*!" to make clear that she harbored no secret dream of re-annexation.

I nodded to indicate that I understood.

"*Ich bin auch*...I too am"—she hesitated a moment—"*das Kind von Flüchtlinge*...the child of refugees."

It was the way she said *Kind*...*child* that made the years fall away from her face and gave her voice the candor of innocence.

"I come," she blinked, embarrassed and proud, "from a long line of Prussian aristocrats, the landed gentry of Poznań, Posen, as it was called back then.

"The War was practically over. The Russians were advancing from the East. It was a winter so bitter and cold the children broke the icicles from the windowsills and sucked them like candy. A decorated tank commander in the *Wehrmacht* who'd been away a long time, and whom the family thought dead, miraculously broke through enemy lines, and came rolling up in his Panzer in the dark of night to the family estate."

She described what followed in vivid detail, like an eyewitness, yet with a certain distance in the telling, like she couldn't decide whether to embrace it or hold it at arm's length.

"The officer leapt out in his neatly pressed uniform, in which the War hadn't made a wrinkle, tipped his cap, which he wore at a jaunty tilt, hugged his two sons and his trembling wife, who took him for a ghost."

She paused to mimic the hollow look in his eyes.

"That night the officer told his wife he wanted to make a blond-haired, blue-eyed daughter.

"'Are you mad?' his wife protested in a whisper, not wanting to wake the children. 'The War is lost, we already have two sons to raise. Why bring another child into this world?'

"But the officer insisted, and his wife dared not refuse a decorated hero of the Reich."

Turning away, the theologian's wife bowed her head to mark a private moment, shut her eyes tight and seemed to be peering inwards, straining, as I suddenly fathomed, to remember the moment of her own conception.

"Bright and early the next day," she continued, her voice now taking on a strange solemnity, "Father put on his perfectly pressed uniform, set the cap on his head at just the right angle, pausing briefly in front of Mother's vanity mirror to approve his appearance, said he'd only be a minute, and as Mother watched from the bedroom window, he smiled, patted the protruding cannon, lifted the hatch, climbed in, set the great metal elephant in motion, and poking his head out, waving to her at the window one last time, leapt out and hurled himself under the rolling tread."

They cleared the table and brought in the dessert, a wild berry parfait that neither of us touched.

"Did she mourn for him?" I inquired.

"There was no time for mourning," my tablemate shook her head. "With the Russian artillery thundering ever closer all through the day and into the night, Mother pulled herself together, took a pickax, buried Father's remains, and fled with the clothes on her back and a small bundle, with my brothers in tow, and the seed of a child planted in her womb, walking all the way to Berlin.

"Father posthumously had his wish, a blond-haired, blue-eyed daughter," she shrugged, with a look that wavered between disapproval and a proud affirmation of self. "The four of us lived together in a cramped attic room with a ceiling through which it rained and snowed. In that leaky attic I grew up with barely enough space to stretch my arms and legs, but there," she smiled, "I felt protected.

"When I grew up I met and married my husband"— she nodded at the theologian, who cast increasingly concerned looks to see his wife so stirred up with a stranger, to which she replied with reassuring nods. "I became a kindergarten teacher, had a long career, and just retired last year."

She was horrified, she said, at the number of broken families her pupils came from, one in three in Germany. She hoped to devote her "golden years"—the hackneyed expression took on a freshness framed by her radiant, tightly braided blond head—volunteering to help children in need.

I had stuck around too long to escape the economist's lecture, but I was preoccupied and don't remember a word of what he said about the present crisis or his prognosis for the future.

I kept glancing at the theologian's wife, now seated beside her husband, her hand in his. Born of conflicting legends, we were bound in braided tragedies. And though I still can't fathom what it means to feel protected, and doubt I ever will, as disparate as our destinies are, there is an undeniable parallel between the motorcycle that carried my father to one kind of freedom and the tank that took her father to another, on both of which history hitched a ride.

II

The Other Germany

Travel Notes from the Far Side
of the Wall

Life and times in the former German Democratic Republic, observed in fleeting glimpses during a short

trip taken there in 1986, have since changed dramatically. Many of the ruins in Berlin, Dresden, and elsewhere have been razed or renovated. Smiles are more widespread today, but so are disappointment, unemployment, and its insidious byproduct, flare-ups of political extremism. But the memories of what was remain a vivid backdrop to the present. So it seemed appropriate to follow the preceding portrait of Berlin with a peek at the way things were in the rest of the country before the Wall came down. (Note: The fiancée referred to below is now my wife.)

AUGUST 13, 1986, MARKED THE TWENTY-FIFTH ANNI-versary of the building of the Berlin Wall, and we were on the far side, in the East visiting friends.

Yellow jackets hum and hover lackadaisically around abandoned, half-empty paper cups and spilt pools of a nondescript bubbly yellow drink. The tables haven't been cleared or wiped for hours, days perhaps. A printed sign on the kiosk advertises coffee, but a handwritten addendum advises that the coffee machine is temporarily out of order. After a few exploratory sips of the tepid yellow liquid, the only refreshments to be had, we decide to leave it to the insects, as countless others have wisely done before us.

It is Saturday morning, almost noon, and the nearby facades of a defunct bakeshop and a deserted restaurant look rather like the sagging movie set of a low-budget World War II movie long after the final take. It is difficult to conceive that the outdoor café in which we are seated (the key attraction of which from our point of view is its chairs) is located in the heart of East Berlin, just across the street from the S-Bahn terminal, the border crossing at Friedrichstraße Station.

We are an hour early for our rendezvous with Werner. My fiancée Claudie and I take turns going back to peruse the crowd inside the station. She has never met my friend, but knows his face from a photograph. In the waiting area there is an atmosphere of subdued anticipation, none of the electricity, the manic energy that charges big city airports and train stations in the West. People lean like wilted flowers, like the girls not picked at a dance, looking every now and then with a sad mix of hope and despair, while visitors and relatives trickle in from the West.

My turn to sit it out now in the café while she looks for Werner. Why am I here?

It hit me the moment we landed at Tegel Airport in West Berlin, and I heard the first imperious syllables over the loudspeaker: "*BITTE ZU BEACHTEN…!*" ("Please observe…!"), and the wave of love and revulsion that I feel for everything German swept over me with a fury. It is difficult to explain this to my French wife-to-be, for whom German is the language of the philosophers, and Germans are fellow Europeans with a common penchant for abstract thinking. There is nothing abstract about my feelings for this place, its people, or the sound of the language with its sublime mix of chiseled consonants and guttural intensity.

To me, the American-born son of Austrian-Jewish refugees, German is and always will be my mysterious code of displacement, the secret language "we" use when "we" don't want "them" to understand. That there is a place where "they" also speak it, is a fact as disturbing to me as it is exciting; for here, imagination and reality meet, private is public and nightmare thoughts surface as easily as bubbles in a carbonated drink.

A yellow jacket is drowning in my cup, its tiny wings

fluttering desperately, stirring up the fizz of its imminent death—if I save it, it'll sting me for sure.

I am anxious about this reunion with Werner. Will we have anything to say to each other, or will the next seven days be a strained rehashing of a moment's communion eleven years ago?

★

Warsaw, 1975, I was there ostensibly doing research for a book the subject of which never seemed to materialize. Saturday afternoon found me at the State Jewish Theatre, one half of an audience of two. There were earphones for those who required translation from Yiddish, I didn't, and the bearded young man, the other half of the audience, asked me, first in halting Polish, no response, then in German, if I understood the language of the play.

"Yes and no," I said.

A student of Catholic theology, as I later learned, Werner had just stopped short of becoming a priest. We talked over Russian tea and cigarettes: a Jew and a German, a would-be author and a priest gone astray. He loved Poland, he said, because he felt freer here than back home in East Germany.

"Germany and Poland, it's all one big cemetery to me," I admitted bluntly, with the kind of candor one can only permit oneself with complete strangers and intimate friends.

Werner had since become the director of an old age home, gotten married, to a Polish woman of course, and fathered two children. "I can't travel," he wrote to me on Warsaw Pact paper, "and it's a shame that we should never see each other again. Why don't you come and visit us?"

★

Two soldiers stroll by carrying large spherical objects under their arms, which on closer inspection, reveal themselves to be watermelons, rarities in a country where collective farming produces a limited harvest, the best of which is reserved for export. The soldiers are drunk and sway with the weight of the melons. The melons are large and round, and because they are a similar tint of green to the soldiers' caps and uniforms, they look (as the soldiers recede in the distance and I watch them from the rear) as if they are carrying their heads in their hands. Are they watching me? I wonder.

★

Yesterday, in West Berlin, at a friend's loft overlooking the River Spree and the Wall, I stood transfixed at the window, eyeing the East German patrol boats motoring by below. The guards pulled out their binoculars and I pulled out my camera, and for an instant we were glued to each other's sights, in the tenuous intimacy of interlocked looks. Christoph, who has lived with that view for the last ten years, has never been to East Berlin. "I have only to stick my hand out the window and my fingertips already touch the Wall," he scowls. "Why put my foot there too?!"

Although it is a relatively easy matter for anyone to visit East Berlin for the day, most West Berliners would rather not. Ask them why and you get a vague answer, something about the inconvenience and the effort involved—a little like the response you might get from a Manhattanite asked to visit the Bronx. There is a good dose of fear shrouded beneath a tongue-in-cheek scorn. "I'd like to reserve the same room for when we return," I said to the owner of the little hotel off the Kurfürstendamm where we spent the night. "*If* you return!" he grinned, twirling the edges of his handlebar mustache.

★

A dream last night: we were arrested by a faceless border guard perched like a bird of prey on the Wall. "What a shame," I protest, "with so precious few of the Chosen People left, surely, the remainder merit special treatment!" He nods in agreement, and I realize suddenly that "special treatment," ("*Sonderbehandlung*" in German), an infamous euphemism of the forties, can have fatal repercussions.

This morning's border crossing was, in fact, anticlimactically quick and uneventful: a mere matter of passport photos checked against faces, entry fees paid, and rubber stamps pounded against paper. No one even challenged the chin beard I had grown since the picture was taken—the gall of them not to notice!

★

"I recognized him immediately from the photograph," Claudie insists, as I embrace my old friend, and squint at the bald-headed stranger with the glassy eyes. There are two men standing there before me instead of one. "This is Father B.," Werner introduces his companion. "He is visiting us from Lithuania." Do I detect a hint of warning in his voice, or is it nervousness?

"I have the books," I whisper, precious contraband from the West. The other man has struck up a conversation with Claudie, but seems to be listening in on ours.

"Thank you," says Werner with a strained smile clouding his otherwise clear, open face, a smile in which I read a further note of caution.

"I am pleased much to meet you," the priest says in broken German, extending his hand.

Now I am convinced of it: "*They*" have put my friend under surveillance, and have sent this agent along to keep tabs on him and his visitors from the West.

We walk along the famous avenue, Unter den Linden, past somber gray embassies and ministries; Werner nods up toward a rotating camera overhead: "Big Brother is watching you," he jokes.

Later that evening, the Lithuanian priest and I tap glasses and laugh at my suspicion. While First Party Secretary Erich Honecker is gathering his minions in East Berlin for a rousing pep talk and a rattling of arms in commemoration of the twenty-fifth anniversary of the erection of the "Anti-Fascist Protective Rampart," we gather for another kind of occasion. It is Werner's thirty-ninth birthday, and he and his wife Joanna have invited some friends over to celebrate. The first order of business is eating.

A huge pot of *bigos*, a Polish meat and cabbage stew that has been simmering for three days, spreads its beguiling scent. Everyone takes a plateful, leaving room for the caviar, the deviled eggs, cold meat and sausage, and the red and yellow tomatoes from Joanna's garden.

German beer and Russian vodka loosen tongues. The mood is warm and lighthearted.

"How do they take X-rays in Moscow?" one guest inquires.

"That's easy," another replies, "just prop up your patient in between two citizens of Chernobyl and watch him glow."

"There's a race to the moon," a third guest begins, before we have even had time to digest the previous punch line, "the Russians get there first, and what do they do? They take out their buckets and brushes and start painting it, red of course. Now the Americans get wind of the scheme via satellite. Congress is in an uproar. Send up a rocket filled with vats of white paint, the Republicans demand. But the Democrats have a better idea. Just let Ivan do all the work, they say, let him paint the whole moon red, all we have to do is slap on a Coca-Cola insignia."

We are a motley crew seated facing each other in a

circle, in a living room overlooking the Polish border, in Frankfurt an der Oder, sixty miles east of the Berlin Wall. Our company includes: a mathematician wearing a SAVE THE WHALES T-shirt his cousin sent him from the West; his wife, a chemist, draped in a brightly colored Indian cotton dress; a visiting Hungarian student brandishing a pocket dictionary to bolster his rather rudimentary German; an anti-conformist collarless German priest with a penchant for frank words and red wine; an erudite cook of scholarly inclination; a Czech teacher on vacation; the soft-spoken Lithuanian priest I mistook for a member of the secret police; Werner, and his Polish wife; my French fiancée, a college professor by profession, and myself, a Jewish-American writer of Austrian extraction and ambivalent emotions.

Is this the Germany I love or the Germany I hate, the home of fairy tale magic or the black art of asphyxiation?

The priest reaches for his guitar, the teacher pulls out his harmonica and I am swept back to a scene from the sixties, the idealism still intact, yet with none of the false naïveté—here everybody knows the score—and no need for drugs to get us any higher.

What do you sing under such circumstances?

You start with the song that everyone knows: Claudie shrinks back in her chair; it is hard to be French and have to hear the hundredth rendition of "Frère Jacques," a chorus sung in everyone's native tongue. Even she has to smile, moved despite herself at the eternal international appeal of the simple, banal lyrics and melody, surely the hit tune of all time.

When the priest concludes "Das Lindenbaum Rag," a raucous honky-tonk burlesque on the Schubert classic, clears his throat with a swallow of wine, and launches into Schiller's "Die Gedanken Sind Frei" (Thoughts Are Free), the words, set to Beethoven's music, have a powerful, and under the circumstances, subversive ring.

Yet neither Werner nor his friends would ever think of themselves as dissidents. All observant Catholics, and as such, members of a subculture, an island of alternative thinking tolerated, if frowned upon, by the atheist state, they are also firm believers in the fundamental precepts of Socialism. This is their home, and for all its material limitations, one can lead a quiet happy life here. Healthcare is free, unemployment unknown, no bag ladies or beggars haunt the streets. For better and for worse, the state takes care of its citizens. What infuriates Werner and his friends is not the ideology of the system, but the suffocating sense of being cut off from the outside world and the oppressive impositions of a government bureaucracy riddled with inconsistencies.

The sight of a huge T.V. antenna on every rooftop within broadcast distance of the border may not at first surprise the visitor from the West, until it is pointed out that no one here even bothers to watch the local programs with their tedious emphasis on progress in farm and factory. It is, of course, illegal to tune in to West German T.V., but everyone who can, does. This fact of life is tacitly accepted to such an extent that the official East German nightly news broadcast includes commentary on events (the nuclear accident at Chernobyl, for instance) reported only on the Western channels.

But what the state fears far more than the seductive, albeit pacifying, allure of electronically transmitted images, are the insidious, long-lasting effects of uncontrolled exposure to the printed word.

★

Perusing the offerings at a bookstore, I am at first amazed at the apparent profusion of literature and the crowd of would-be buyers. Books are clearly a prized commodity in the German Democratic Republic; this is a country where people still read. Avid bibliophiles are apprized far in advance of the appearance of new editions, and because of limited printing runs, popular books disappear almost as fast as they hit the shelves.

"Look," says Claudie, "they even have Kafka!" I am surprised, downright flabbergasted, to find that sage, melancholy face greeting me here of all places. But the irony is almost too good, too Kafkaesque to be true: for the title I had first read as *Sämtliche Schriften* (Complete Writings) turns out on closer examination to be *Amtliche Schriften* (Administrative Writings), a compendium, not of his elusive parables, but of the official reports and letters he prepared on the job for the insurance company and the government institute, the two mundane masters to whom he sacrificed his daylight hours and whom he cursed in his diaries at night.

"Yes," the store attendant tells us, "other works by the author have been published." "No," she regrets to inform us, "they are not currently available, they are unfortunately out of print."

Indeed, the printed word serves an important function in a country in which billboards preach eternal

progress and bliss. But slogans like EVERYTHING FOR THE
GOOD OF THE PEOPLE, FOR THE HAPPINESS OF THE NATION!
have a hollow ring: they lack the polish of western corporate masterpieces of indoctrination (like General
Electric's PROGRESS IS OUR MOST IMPORTANT PRODUCT);
the People here are not convinced.

On a streetcar in Dresden we discovered an inge-
nious bit of graffiti. The plaque on the window ledge
that is supposed to warn NICHT HINAUSLEHNEN! (Don't
lean out!), has had several letters skillfully excised by
an anonymous hand, and warns instead: NICHT HIN
S EHN! (Don't look!). No one, we are told, reads the
propaganda-filled columns of the official newspapers,
except for the news of local interest, the birth and death
announcements on the last page. And no one seems
to pay much attention to the billboard slogans either,
which is not to say that illusions don't run rampant, illusions of another sort.

★

"*Da drüben!*" (Over there!) Ingrid, one of Werner's
friends, laments wistfully, her voice on the edge of
tears, as if conjuring up an image of paradise lost and

172

irretrievable on the other side of the Wall. "Why won't they let us travel there? Why do they treat us like children!?" The West to her, as to many of her countrymen, is one part fact and nine parts fable. It is the great beyond they see pictures of on T.V., the promised land of plenty, mythic configuration, fantasies of which can make a mature adult burn with infantile rage.

We are seated together, sipping tea at the asylum where Werner's wife, Joanna, serves as a psychologist, and where her friend Ingrid works as a physical therapist. In the morning, when we arrived, the patients, mostly women and girls between the ages of fifteen and fifty, swarmed around us, some touching us cautiously, some running up to hug us, some staring bemused from afar. Ingrid and six other therapists teach them the rudiments of weaving and woodworking. The work demands infinite patience and boundless reserves of sympathy akin to love. Ingrid herself has no children. Her husband, an anesthesiologist, is leaving shortly to spend a year in Nicaragua, to help build a new hospital for the Sandinistas. It is neither humanitarianism nor a dedication to socialism that drove him to volunteer, Ingrid insists, but the chance to get out, to travel and see something of the world. Ingrid fears that he will never come back.

"You don't, you can't understand what it means to be locked in!" she cries, glaring at us for an instant, then shaking her head, as if to beg forgiveness.

True, we cannot understand, we who come from the West, stay a few days, then travel on elsewhere, to other picturesque places. Ours is the license to come and go as we please.

Together we tour the grounds of the asylum, the workshops and the wards with their neat and tidy little cubicles, each cheerfully furnished with curtains, cupboard, and beds. Claudie unwittingly shuts the hall door behind us, the bolt falls electronically into place and for ten long minutes we have an inkling of what it means to be locked in. When finally an attendant hears our pounding and opens the door, we stagger out into the yard, still shaking from our little taste of claustrophobic terror. A teenage girl with dark, penetrating eyes runs over to Joanna, hugging her close. "Please! Please!" she cries, "Take me with you!" She will not let go and the attendant has to gently pry open her fiercely locked fingers.

★

"Our guests are friends from America and France," Werner explains to the twelve old women gathered in the lounge of the old age home of which he is director: "You can ask them any questions you like." The women study us with an assortment of smiles and scowls, their curious eyes scuttling about like beetles trapped beneath thick lenses.

"Is it true," the boldest woman begins, addressing herself to Claudie, "that Mireille Mathieu isn't married yet?" Not being up on the private lives of French pop singers, my fiancée confesses her ignorance in this matter; the women are visibly disappointed. Other questions about crime and violence and the treatment of old people in the West are more easily answered, with no attempt made on our part to paint a rosy picture.

"How is it," the bold one inquires, "that the young gentleman speaks such good German?"

What shall I tell them of my heritage, why "*Angst*" rings truer to my ear than "fear," and "*Tod*" echoes darker than "death," and why I cannot look an aging German in the eye without wondering what he or she was doing back *then*?

"My parents come from Vienna," I explain. "Jewish refugees," I add, to set the record straight.

"*Ach ja*," one woman speaks for the rest, "it was terrible what happened to those poor people."

"Did you know any Jews before the War?" I ask.

"Oh yes," the same woman replies, "there were Jewish girls in my class in school, we did everything together."

"Remember Hirsch's Department Store?" another woman recalls, setting off a wave of nostalgic sighs. "He was a gem of a man, old Hirsch," she smiles, remembering, "always seated at the door, always greeting you politely as you entered. And the things you could buy there! In the old days, nothing like the dull, drab window displays today!" The other women nod and mutter their agreement.

"Of course when you entered a Jewish store, you know, the Jew wouldn't let you leave without buying something," the bold one interrupts.

"How did he force you to buy?" I ask.

"He had his ways," she insinuates. I let it pass.

"What happened to Hirsch?" I ask.

"There was the boycott,[7] you know," the woman who had first conjured up the ghost of old Hirsch explains,

---

[7] The Nazi boycott of Jewish enterprises called on April 1, 1933, the first official act of the Nazi government directed against the Jews.

"and Mode Mueller—that was the Aryan competition—wasn't he ever pleased!"

"He was a 'White Jew,' that one," another woman comments, "a real swindler!"

"Did anyone continue buying at Hirsch's despite the boycott?" I ask.

"In the beginning, yes," the first woman replies, "but then my husband said, Lisl, think of my position—he was next in line for assistant postmaster!—so I had to stop going there, what else could I do!"

"What happened to Hirsch?" I ask again.

"He disappeared—we heard terrible stories—who could believe them?" she shrugs her shoulders. More sighs and silence all around.

"But we had it bad too, you know," the bold woman blurts out: "Better not to remember!"

★

Like space, time too is divided and strangely disjointed here, split between an unhappy past and an uncertain present. Walk the streets of small town and big city alike, and you are struck by the jarring appearance of once splendid, now crumbling villas still pockmarked with forty-year-old bullet holes and craters, as if the War had ended just yesterday and the authorities hadn't quite yet gotten around to repairs. The scaffolding holding the walls in place is itself in many cases quite rickety, and the few buildings that have been rebuilt, some even restored to their former splendor, emphasize, by contrast, the miserable condition of the rest. No cosmetic surgery has excised the scars of war, no flood of dollars has assuaged the pain of defeat.

★

Dresden is a striking case in point. The city once lauded as the "German Prague," before the Allied bombing of February 13, 1945, reduced it to rubble, still gives evidence of bygone glory. The few palaces left standing, now graying with age, that line the quay along the River Elbe, present an imposing vista of eighteenth-century pomp. But step back into the heart of the old city, and you are surrounded by ruins. It is hard to fathom that these monumental brick arches and charred regal facades, though cordoned off and enshrined with the reverence usually accorded antiquities, are the product of recent ravage.

I am photographing the skeletal remains of the Frauenkirche (Church of Our Lady), starkly silhouetted against the twilight sky, and an old man materializes out of nowhere.

"Tragic, isn't it," he remarks. "The Americans and the British did this, you know." I nod uneasily. "Where are you from?" he inquires.

"New York," I swallow, expecting the worst.

"American!?" he gasps, studying me from head to foot; the incarnation of the inconceivable. And then, with regret instead of rancor: "What a pity you let Ivan get here before you!"

★

Looking down from the hilltop bedecked by Gothic castle and cathedral, surveying the helter-skelter array of steep red rooftops and narrow cobblestone streets, it is easy to imagine a Rapunzel letting down her hair here or a Rumpelstilzchen stamping his tiny feet behind one of the garret windows: Meißen is the model fairy tale town; even Walt Disney could not have done better. Just one giant step upriver from Dresden—twenty minutes by train—this little haven of once upon a time is far removed from the grim realities of the twentieth century. Its restaurants serve fine food and the local white wine, its bakeshops conjure up delectable cakes, its famous porcelain workshops turn out delicate and costly antique-style figurines and plates. This is a Germany that almost transcends geographic partition and temporal disjunction. Here even an American traveler can forget, or at least momentarily suspend, the traumatic dimension of his German-Jewish roots. He can let his fantasy languish in a childhood reverie not yet corrupted by history; follow the bread crumbs strewn by Hänsel and Gretel all the way to a gingerbread house, almost but not quite forgetting, even as he nibbles on its sweet foundation—the walnut torte is delicious, or perhaps you prefer the mocha cream—that the oven within was not used only for baking cake.

*

In Leipzig, between trains, we take in the magnificent St. Thomas Church—where Johann Sebastian Bach performed his fugues, where his mellifluous organ still stands on display, and where the master himself lies buried—and the little synagogue across the river in the old ghetto, nestled in an alleyway, invisible from the street. Spared for mercenary reasons, because of the surrounding apartments, the synagogue was transformed into a soap factory during the War, and only recently renovated and restored at state expense. Its caretaker is a gaunt man of indeterminate age, his leathery face etched with the cuneiform of painful memory. Like the building he watches over, he and the thirty-nine other Jews who still live in Leipzig are an afterthought, a sad postscript.

"Now everyone wants to be our friend," he says with a bitter smile. "I remember when they gathered the old people and pushed them into the river, and those who could swim were later put on the trains…anti-Semitism today? Oh no," he laughs, "there are no Nazis, never were any Nazis here…"

Later, at the train station, with five minutes to spare, I am standing facing a wall in the men's room, a stranger on either side, with no partition to offer even the semblance of privacy, my circumcised identity hanging prone between my legs.

The sky is gray overhead as the S-Bahn rolls into Oranienburg, a dingy outlying district of East Berlin, whose one claim to fame is the site of the former concentration camp Sachsenhausen, now a state museum. The clouds explode as if on cue, letting fall a barrage of rain and what, were it not August, I'd swear from the sting of it is hail. A run-down beer garden with a few umbrella-covered tables offers a modest shelter. As usual here in the East, the menu recommends various choices, but the actual offerings are limited to beer and Wurst. The Wurst is hot at least and the beer is cold. It is early afternoon and the clientele appear, from the look of them, to have consumed a good deal of the latter. One particularly red-faced souse, who has been eyeing my camera and foreign-cut clothes, saunters over, sits himself down beside me and slams his beer mug down on the table. "Hey you, take my picture!" he demands, twisting his mouth into a hybrid grimace-grin. "You Fascist-Socialist!" he hisses, and breaks into a sodden laugh. The insult stings, though its meaning eludes me.

At the museum, a placard bemoans in bold white letters on a bright red background "the sacrifice of our brothers, fellow fighters and friends." "With deep reverence," the placard concludes, "we honor our cherished dead…"

In death, we are one. Thus the German Democratic Republic lays generous claim to the spiritual estate of the victims; all the killers, it seems, come from the other side of the Wall.

★

It is our last night in the East and friends have gathered again at Werner's to see us off. The wine flows in abundance, the conversation shuttles between subjects: from the alternating chill and thaw of East-West relations and the global politics of the present to the Waldheim Affair and conflicting ruminations on the past.

"For me, for us," Ulrike maintains, "it is difficult to feel anything about *those times*." An intense young woman with short cropped hair and serious gray eyes, she pauses to weigh her words. "We know intellectually that we ought to feel," she says, "but the feeling just isn't there."

Stroking his apostolic red beard, Karl disagrees: "As schoolchildren, we all had to visit Buchenwald; we brought along our transistor radios to drown out the teacher's words; the experience meant nothing to us. But then at eighteen," he recounts, "I paid a second compulsory visit to the concentration camp, this time with my platoon, a brand new army recruit. We were supposed to feel proud: they told us we were the defenders of peace, the rightful heirs to the brave resistance against 'Hitler-Fascism.' But all I felt was shame to be standing there in that place in a German uniform. I wanted to crawl into a deep hole and die."

Johannes, on the other hand, rejects any sense of shame or guilt, yet at fifteen, for some reason still a mystery to him, he climbed on his bicycle and rode all the way to Sachsenhausen, knowing full well where he was headed. "And when my children get older, old enough to understand," he says, "I will take them there too."

★

As Claudie and I ride the elevated S-Bahn back across the border and pass once again over the Wall, another parapet comes to mind. In Jerusalem, Jews from around the world come to lean in the shadow of the Wailing Wall, feeling the pangs of exile and the comfort of return, and here in Berlin, a modern rampart carves the

German nation in two, inflicting memory. Funny that we both have our walls.

ACKNOWLEDGMENTS

This book draws primarily on the author's experiences during a memorable stay as a Holtzbrinck Fellow in 2010 at the American Academy in Berlin, to whose director, Gary Smith, its staff and trustees, in particular, Stefan von Holtzbrinck, he remains eternally grateful. An early draft of the foreword appeared, in German translation, under the title "Ich berlinisiere, also bin ich," in *Die Welt*, July 1, 2010. The brief reflection that would become the chapter "Of Sublime Ecstasy and Guttural Disgust: My German Language" originated as an essay titled "Double-Take: The Bilingual Family," in *Family, A Celebration*, an anthology edited by Margaret Campbell, published by Peterson's, Princeton, N.J., in 1995. A first draft of the chapter "Wurst Lust" appeared on the website Mr. Beller's Neighborhood (mrbellersneighborhood. com). An abbreviated version of the chapter "Protected" first ran in *Habitus, a Diaspora Journal,* 2011; the text in its entirety was subsequently selected for *The Best Travel Writing 2011,* Travelers' Tales, thereafter issued, in German translation, as "Die Frau des Theologen," in the April 2011 issue of *Cicero, Magazin für politische Kultur*; and finally honored with the Gold Grand Prize for Best Travel Story of the Year in 2012 in the Solas Awards. "The Other Germany: Travel Notes from the Far Side of the Wall," was originally published in the journal *Jewish Frontiers,* in 1989. The author also wishes to thank James O'Reilly and Christy Quinto for their astute editorial acumen.

ABOUT THE AUTHOR

Photo by Jean-Luc Fievet

A writer in multiple modes in English and German, Peter Wortsman has been dubbed "a twentieth-century Brother Grimm" (*Bloomsbury Review*) and "a delinquent Hans Christian Andersen" (by playwright Mark O'Donnell). He is the author of a book of short fiction, *A Modern Way To Die* (1991); two stage plays, *The Tattooed*

Man Tells All (2000) and *Burning Words* (2004); an artists' book, *it-t=i* (2005), on which he collaborated with his brother, artist Harold Wortsman, comprising Peter's poetry and his brother's etchings; and a novel, *Cold Earth Wanderers* (forthcoming 2014). Also a critically-acclaimed translator from the German, his English takes on German classics include *Posthumous Papers of a Living Author*, by Robert Musil, now in its third edition (1987, 1995, and 2006—and excerpted in *Flypaper*, 2011); *Travel Pictures*, by Heinrich Heine (2008); *Selected Prose of Heinrich von Kleist* (2010); *Selected Tales of the Brothers Grimm* (2013); and *Tales of the German Imagination, From the Brothers Grimm to Ingeborg Bachmann*, an anthology he also compiled (2013).

His travel writing has appeared in major newspapers and websites, and was selected five years in a row (2008-2012) for *The Best Travel Writing* series. He is the recipient of the Beard's Fund Short Story Award and the Geertje Potash-Suhr SCALG-Prosapreis, a prize for short original fiction in German, awarded by the Society for Contemporary American Literature in German. A former fellow of the Fulbright and Thomas J. Watson Foundations, in 2010 he was the Holtzbrinck Fellow at the American Academy in Berlin, where he wrote much of *Ghost Dance in Berlin*. An excerpt from the book won the 2012 Gold Grand Prize for Best Travel Story of the Year in the Solas Awards for Best Travel Writing.